I Will Remember You

Cover Photo, courtesy of Sue Steuart

Marisa, daughter-in-law of Sue and Bernie Steuart
with a young friend from El Salvadore.

Back Cover Photo by Ryan Ford

I Will Remember You

A testament to both tenderness of the human heart and the strength of the human soul

by

Fran Ford

Windswept Press
Interlaken, New York
1994

ISBN: 1–55787–120–5
Library of Congress Catalog Number 94–60560
Manufactured in the United States of America

A *quality* publication by
Heart of the Lakes Publishing
Interlaken, New York 14847

Dedicated

To all volunteers

Acknowledgments

I am indebted to the entire staff at Catholic Charities. Especially director Pam Wilson for all her help in programming the computer for my use and her unselfish time in support of my endeavor. My deep gratitude to Steve Patnode, office manager, for his patience, his sense of humor, and invaluable assistance in editing and proofreading the final version.

My special thanks to Janet Rock and Suzanne Moore for their time spent in editing. With appreciation to my son Stephen, Mary Fogarty, and Richard W. Ward for their contributions.

Last but not least, my thanks to a special lady, Margot Zeglis, who suggested and had unwavering faith in my writing of this book.

Preface

Plattsburgh, a city of 22,000, is located in rural Clinton County, New York. Its people are descendants of French and English who hold fast to their conservative values and morals. Located in the upper Northeastern corner of New York State, and sixty miles south of Montréal, Québec, Canada, Plattsburgh is known as a tourist and college town. It also is home of the United States Air Force 380th Bombardment Wing. Located on the western shore of Lake Champlain, Plattsburgh is host to the Mayor's Cup sailboat competition each July, drawing people and competitors not only from the neighboring state of Vermont but Canada as well. The State University of New York at Plattsburgh has an excellent hockey team (the Cardinals), making for exciting winter entertainment for loyal Plattsburgh fans. But in the final months of 1986, the normal events of the city were set aside in a way that touched the everyday lives of the residents of Plattsburgh. The city became internationally known, its people the international story, as they found themselves responding to the needs of those fleeing from human atrocities occurring around the world.

Canada always had its door open to the persecuted of other countries, but in 1986 the United States had passed the Immigration Reform and Control Act concerning undocumented aliens within its borders. This meant illegals living within the United States had to prove by rental receipts, paycheck stubs or other acceptable evidence that they had been here five years prior to May 1986 in order to receive the amnesty offered by the government, or they would face deportation. Many could not, or were distrustful, and sought refuge in Canada before the act became law and was enforced as of May 1987. With the act being passed and countries around the globe being torn by conflict within, Canada soon found itself understaffed to process the increase in applicants seeking refuge. A "change of policy" resulted. Canada closed its border. The claimants had to wait outside Canada's border until their assigned hearing date.

The brunt of the refugees returning to the City of Plattsburgh fell on the Plattsburgh Community Crisis Center, where emergency food, housing, and medical care were given out. Seeing the resources of the agency being drained by the scores of refugees arriving weekly, director Brian Smith turned to the local community. His community had to be made aware of a possible developing tragedy and other agencies had to be involved.

Plattsburgh became a lifeline for the world's homeless. As the call went out to the community for help, some locals, like me, gave hesitatingly at first and then opened their hearts to these strangers. They soon dispelled the harbored fears brought by the difference in race, the difference in language, and the difference in culture. They were human beings struggling to survive in a place not of their choosing.

It was from the middle of December 1986 through early January 1987 that I became aware through the media about the foreign people ending up on the streets of Plattsburgh. It was back in November 1986 that Brian Smith, director of the Crisis Center, saw the refugees returning to Plattsburgh from the Canadian border. With Crisis Center resources being drained, he turned to Jeanie Roberts, director of the American Red Cross, and Rose Pandozy, Commissioner of Clinton County Social Services.

Brian, Jeanie, and Sue Vann, a representative from Social Services, went to the Canadian Immigration Office at Blackpool, Québec, where they learned for the first time about the "change" in Canadian policy. They realized that shortly there was going to be a great impact on Plattsburgh.

Brian, Jeanie and Rose held meetings every Friday at noon, from November 1986 to January 1987, on how to deal with the growing problem and how to fund the growing cost. Brian and Jeanie went on speaking engagements to raise monies, and also to get the word out on the ever-increasing problem. They soon realized these funds would not last or go far towards the cost of food, housing or medical care. They had to make the community aware and get other agencies involved.

The international people, mostly Central Americans, were finding themselves stranded here due to the increase of applicants for refugee status, resulting in a Canadian "change of policy." An additional factor could have been the repercussion from the 1986 Act passed by the United States Congress, which was to go into effect in May 1987.

Before these changes had taken place the people of Plattsburgh were unaware of the internationals passing through on Greyhound buses from New York City to Montréal. Canada soon found itself understaffed to handle the 15 to 30 people that arrived each day at the port of entry, Blackpool, just north of Plattsburgh. Another busy port of entry was near Buffalo, for claimants going to Toronto, Ontario.

In late January the Salvation Army had opened its soup kitchen to feed the displaced, but the numbers grew with each passing day. On February 20, 1987, Canada closed its border, forcing all refugee claimants to wait up to six weeks outside of its border before being allowed to enter for their hearing date. The directors and chairpersons of agencies in Plattsburgh—Crisis Center, Social Services, American Red Cross, Salvation Army, Catholic Charities, Interfaith Council, United Way, Civil Defense, and Clinton County Legislators and City Fathers—met on how to handle the needs facing

11

our community. The city had never coped with an influx of such a multitude of problems and each day they grew. The dire need for money, clothing, medical assistance, food and shelter, without using funds allocated for the local needy, was a great dilemma. Even if the agencies could help it would not be nearly enough, so they turned to Washington for help and were denied. It was not a problem to be dealt with federally, but rather locally.

On February 23rd, the Salvation Army opened a temporary shelter in its gym. Health care now could be dispensed to the refugees, to the great relief of not only the "city fathers," but the general population of Plattsburgh. They did not know what illnesses these people could be carrying, so each day, seven days a week, a public health nurse would visit to attend the sick and health-screen new arrivals.

With bus-loads being returned from the border the situation was becoming more desperate. Refugees were now sleeping on and under the chapel pews in the Salvation Army building. The gym was full. The local news media was putting out calls for Spanish translators, volunteers, clothing and food. The response was extraordinary, with a tractor-trailer load of clothing arriving from Vermont, and boxes of winter clothes, boots, canned and dried foods donated to the Salvation Army. Donations also came from private citizens, local businesses and churches. News of the plight was picked up by NBC on February 26th, with Fred Briggs giving a short report about the immigration problems on the "Today" show.

Pressure on state officials by "city fathers" and directors of agencies to open the National Guard Building on Route 9 North as a second shelter was successful, thereby relieving the overcrowded gym at the Salvation Army Building. A temporary reprieve was achieved for a growing problem.

I Will Remember

Cozy-warm in our middle-class home, my husband John and I discussed the nightly reports regarding the refugee situation. We felt it wasn't our problem. Our own people came first; charity begins at home, as the adage goes. With reports that Commissioner of Social Services Rose Pandozy might be going to Albany to seek help from Governor Cuomo, I remember saying, "Take the illegals with you and deposit them on Cuomo's steps." Yet deep within, it upset me that I had said this even to my husband. I always thought I had compassion and was not prejudiced. Did my reaction occur because the situation was now taking place in my city and not a large city, or in the south, or in some country I had never heard of? I felt I did not judge a person by color, race or religion. After all, thirty years ago, I had married a second-generation Irishman, hadn't I? I remembered my grandfather asking me, "Why are you marrying this foreigner?" My husband was a native from the southern tier of New York State! I laughed many times in retelling this story over the years.

It was March 4, 1987, Ash Wednesday, the beginning of the Holy Season of Lent. As in past years, I was looking forward to attending daily Mass. As a homemaker who knows the meaning of the "empty nest," I always looked forward to this special season of renewal.

Father George W. Tobin, pastor of Saint Mary's of the Lake, Cumberland Head, had a stirring message, but three sentences re-awoke feelings I had felt but denied for months. "Look within yourself these next forty days to help others, the less fortunate. It is not enough to fast or abstain. Give of yourself."

I came home deep in thought. I tuned in our local radio station, WIRY, and Gordie Little was giving a report on the desperate need for volunteers, private cars, drivers or just people to answer telephones. I picked up the local newspaper, the *Press-Republican*. In headlines on the "Local" page, I saw the call for volunteers. Twice I went to the phone, twice I turned away. The third time, I placed the call. I felt I could answer phones, I did not have to associate in any way with these displaced people. Yes, I could just answer phones. I was told to come to Catholic Charities at one o'clock that afternoon. Two hours to ponder, two hours of self-doubt.

The office of Catholic Charities was a pleasant surprise to me. Located in a residential area of Plattsburgh, it has a warm aura of home, with soft lighting, home furnishings and a fireplace. A friendly young man, Steve Patnode, directed me upstairs to a small room with a desk, two chairs, and two small windows, where I met Rev. F. Kingsley Emerson from the First Baptist Church in Plattsburgh. I was greeted with a bright smile and warm handshake. Immediately I felt comfortable as he took my name, address and telephone number. He issued to me a Salvation Army ID card which held his signature. I was about to ask if tomorrow would be OK to start, but I never had the chance. He promptly informed me to proceed to the Salvation Army building and ask for Ginger, who was in charge of dispersing volunteers to where they were needed most.

As I pulled into the parking lot of the Salvation Army I was aware of dark-skinned men, huddled against the brick wall out of the March wind, smoking cigarettes. Collars were pulled high, heads tucked down, seeking what little warmth a lightweight jacket gives. Eyes followed me as I walked toward the entrance, the ground littered with cigarette butts. I opened the door to face wall-to-wall people! Women, men, young and old, milling around, leaning against the wall, or sitting on a floor without enough space. Noise, confusion, with a crying baby somewhere. As I side-stepped and worked my way through the crowd with many "excuse me's" to what resembled an office, I was aware of unfamiliar cooking smells permeating the hall. Three women answered non-stop ringing telephones, as old women stood in the doorway looking on. With deep-lined faces, eyes expressionless, they clutched their torn sweaters, waiting for what? It seemed no one was in charge. I asked for Ginger. One of the ladies answering the telephone introduced herself as Ginger. She asked if I had a car and told me two Hispanic women had to go to the doctor. There went my idea of answering phones! No time to ask questions, it had to be done now. I asked to make a call to my husband at New York State Electric and Gas (NYSEG), for dinner could be late. Ginger left, disappearing into the crowd. When I told John where I was his response was, "What the hell are you doing there?" I was taken aback by his words but forged forward.

"I will explain later when I get home," I replied. This did not go unnoticed by one of the ladies answering phones. "No problem, I hope?" "No," I answered, "Where are the women who need to go to the doctor?"

As I led the women to my car they followed so closely that if I had stopped they would have bumped into me. One spoke broken English, but soon I felt awkward, uncomfortable. I was thankful the doctor's office was close by. We entered the waiting room where I felt all eyes were on us. I took a seat across the room, the farthest chair I could find. Why? Was I embarrassed to be seen with these women that were different in language and appearance? Yes, I was! The ride back to the shelter took place in silence. Ginger told me to report to the second shelter, the National Guard building, tomorrow at 7:30 a.m. Help was desperately needed there and it was closer to my home. Dinner was well underway upon my arrival home at 6 p.m. My husband was somewhat supportive of my efforts upon hearing what I had seen that day.

"Father Tobin, I have taken your message to heart," I said silently. There would be no turning back after today. And so begin my reflections.

Late Winter, 1987

Thursday, March 5

I arrived promptly at 7:30 a.m. as the dawn's bright pink glow suffused the eastern sky. It was bitingly cold as I walked briskly toward a large windowless cinder-block building that was used in part by the National Guard. I entered into a lighted foyer where two soldiers were sitting at a table. What a surprise! In a clipped military tone they asked me what my purpose was in being there. I explained I was with the refugee program and they asked not only for my Salvation Army ID card but my own personal ID. Off to the right I observed a large well-lit office, where in undertones an officer and other soldiers were talking and drinking coffee. I felt I had entered a stockade. I signed their log sheet and was allowed to pass to a smaller, dimly-lit office located directly behind them. A fortyish-looking man wearing a Salvation Army shirt and cap was sitting with his booted feet on a small desk. I was asked again to show the Salvation Army ID as he introduced himself as Bob Davies. The desk held a legal pad, log book and a telephone. Good. This is where I'd be answering the phone, so I thought. Bob told me the director, Mike Brassard, was inside checking on the refugees. Unexpectedly, in the doorway, loomed a tall, burly, bearded man still wearing a knitted toque and his winter coat. There was hardly enough room for the three of us. His voice was soft and gentle in his greeting, expressing his pleasure in seeing me. While removing his hat and coat he explained briefly the operation of the program and went over what needed to be done on a daily basis. (I learned later he was a local businessman giving freely of his time, 16 to 18 hour days, leaving his business in the hands of a manager.) I was told breakfast, consisting of doughnuts and coffee, would be arriving by the Salvation Army van between 9:00-9:30 a.m. He asked me to help him set out paper plates, styrofoam cups, spoons, sugar, and to dispense coffee out of army insulated canisters when it arrived. Also, there would be milk for the babies and children only. I heard stirrings and muffled voices, with the sounds of children's whimpering filtering down the darkened hall. Mike had done wake-up call just before I arrived. Immediately after breakfast he would call names of refugees from a selected list; those who would go for showers at the Young Men's Christian Association (YMCA) and those to do their laundry at a local laundromat if there was time. Several trips would be made in the morning and again in the afternoon. I asked how many refugees were at this location and was told 75 to 80, mostly from Central America. How would it be possible to transport this many each day? I was informed the group was divided and went for showers every third day. Laundry was worked in when time and cars were available. The Salvation Army had one van and that operated out of their building. Mike said he had a van for his business that would be brought to the shelter to be used. In the meantime, he desperately needed drivers with private cars. My God, what a task! "Welcome aboard, Fran," he said with a warm smile. I suddenly realized how much compassion this giant of a man felt and held for "my people," as he lovingly referred to them. I was the first volunteer with a car who was not a member of the Salvation Army that had come to Shelter 2, which opened February 26th.

It was 8:30 a.m. when the phone rang. Mike told me to answer "Shelter 2" and log the time, the caller, and the message. It was Shelter 1. I was told the van was being loaded with breakfast and Kathy with Mervin would ride over with Brad to help for the day. When I asked Bob who they were, he said, "members of the Salvation Army disaster team," which he was as well.

Bob, who had been on duty since 10:00 p.m. the previous night, would have a ride home on the van's return trip to Shelter 1. It had been a long, quiet night for him, not always the case, with no emergencies. He had not been alone all night, as the entrance was guarded, and an armed soldier was posted on "Fire-Watch" and for security in the room housing the refugees. "What am I getting into!," I wondered.

Mike re-appeared. He had been in to see the officer in charge. "Come on, Fran, let's get the supplies set up for breakfast." I followed him down the hall into a glaringly lit dormitory room with an open ceiling, exposed girders, and large hanging heating units. I could hardly believe my eyes! Row upon row of cots next to one another holding partly dressed men, women with babes in their arms, and whimpering children being dressed, some still reluctant to rise and face another day. They had slept between rough army blankets in their everyday clothes. Families, single men and women, all together in row upon row in this huge cement-floored room, speaking in tongues I did not understand. I followed Mike so closely that if he had stopped abruptly I would have bumped into him.

A row of barren tables with boxes stuffed under them lined the far cinder-block wall. It is here I found the supplies used for meals. A young girl in her early twenties with shoulder-length, curly-black hair, dark sparkling eyes and a smile that lit up her whole face, approached Mike. Mike introduced her as his interpreter and "right-hand" helper, Lupe. Though the room was stuffy and warm, she had a scarf wrapped around her neck, and wore a heavy bulky sweater, wool slacks, and footwear of thin socks and tattered open sandals. I felt my uneasiness lift in the presence of this bubbly young lady who spoke so well English.

Lines of partially-dressed men were forming before the lone men's bathroom. Others were tucking their few belongings under cots and making their beds. It now dawned on me that the refugee program was being run on a military regimen. Although the Salvation Army is a religious organization, it is structured militarily. Though I was being assigned work by Catholic Charities, who coordinated the volunteers, I would learn shortly that all agencies, working together, would operate under the Salvation Army umbrella. This meant any shelter would be staffed by a Salvation Army officer or member, who would be in charge of the Salvation Army policy of said shelter, under the local Commander, Captain Jack Holcomb. Mike, our director, was a member of the Advisory Board of the Salvation Army.

The van arrived at 9 a.m. with breakfast. Kathy and Mervin carried in additional paper supplies as refugee men were sent to bring in the large coffee canisters, boxes of doughnuts, and the milk for children. Women and children were served first and then the men. Not a very appetizing nor nutritious meal to start the day. What about the poor babies, toddlers and young children? What do they eat? I wondered, but didn't ask.

Brad told Mike he would come back with the van after he brought Bob home. It would not be needed until lunchtime and so could be used to bring people for showers. Mike asked me, "How many can you put in your car?" I quickly responded, "Six, if we squeeze." "They'll squeeze," Mike replied. Lupe translated to the group what Mike said. People whose names were called were to line up near the door to the hall, where a towel and bar of soap would be given to those who had none. We'd leave in a half hour. A 16–passenger van would become a 20–passenger van, and my car would carry six people. Mike called the YMCA to inform them of the number to expect at about 10:30 a.m.

I went back to the office after storing the supplies under the tables and left the women to cleaning chores. I found Mike talking (with Lupe translating) with a woman who apparently had a problem. I turned to leave, but Mike said, "Stay." In his quiet way he was showing me the many facets one encounters in this program. I found Mike to be strong but fair, kind and loving, giving a hug when needed or wiping a tear. He was all things to these people: mother, father, nurse, leader and protector.

He had legal documents before him. Going through them, he matched dates from a list. This was when I learned these people were not "illegals," for our federal government had agreed with the government of Canada to allow the refugees to stay legally in the United States until their date of entry. They were permitted to enter Canada twenty-four hours before their hearing, date which would take place in the City of Montréal. They could travel legally anywhere in the United States during their waiting period. There would be a refugee leaving tomorrow for his hearing date, and Mike was double-checking so as not to miss anyone that would be leaving soon.

It was decided Brad and Kathy would staff and cover incoming calls while Mervin would drive the van of refugees to the YMCA. Mike went back with "his people" to see to any needs, to talk with the frightened, to reassure them everything would be OK. He and Lupe walked down the hall, side by side, bringing his light of hope to the despairing people.

Everyone had to sign out at the manned guard post, including me. I had two women and four men in the car, but of particular interest was the blond, greenish-blue-eyed young man who spoke English. I learned his name was George, a graduate from the American University of Lebanon, where he had been a member of their undefeated tennis team. I did not know they were still able to play competition tennis in war-torn Lebanon. I sensed he was proud of his accomplishment, and since my sons Stephen and Chris played tennis, our trip of a few miles passed quickly in our discussion of the game and the university.

Mervin had arrived before me and was very agitated about our keeping "these refugees" in sight and in hand. I thought to myself, "Well now, they are human beings and should be treated accordingly." But since I was the new person on the block I quietly directed all the women to the showers (sort of ignoring an apprehensive Mervin), where a local woman gave a bar of soap to a refugee who had forgotten her own. However, while waiting upstairs for all to gather and be counted, a local man made a negative comment to the receptionist about refugees using the facilities of the YMCA, of which he was a member. Did I feel a tinge of anger? Yes I did!

We arrived back at Shelter 2 and everyone signed in. It was time for Mervin to go to Shelter 1 to pick up lunch. Mike asked how it went. When I told him how Mervin seemed a little bossy, he said, "Don't listen to Mervin. Use your own judgement."

Once again I helped to set up for lunch as young men shot basketball hoops in the background. I noticed how clean and neat this large room was now, compared to the chaotic morning. Some men were reading, some women were entertaining small children, while others just sat on cots. For the first time I saw a small room that held a television, table and chairs, where men were playing cards as young people watched TV. How could it be possible to clothe and feed all these homeless people? Surely they were going to become sick!

Lunch arrived, and these hungry beings were ready to feast on lettuce and tomato salad, hot homemade vegetable soup brought in army containers, rice with pieces of chicken, all the bread they could eat, two 30–gallon insulated containers of Kool-Aid and a box of oranges. It was a banquet to them.

My day ended at 2:30 p.m. Mike asked if I could come in at 9 a.m. tomorrow in time for breakfast. Hours would vary from day to day as to when I was needed. It was OK; my time was flexible.

Friday, March 6

Entering the shelter was easier this morning, with no questions, just showing my ID and signing the sheet. I found Mike in the small office speaking on the phone with Shelter 1. It was apparent that only one other person besides Mike and I would be on, but there would be time to go for laundry today. He was worried that many would not have money for the soap and coin machines. I went in to set up for breakfast and on entering the housing area I was greeted with "buenos dias" (good morning). Words did not have to be understood; their warm smiles transcended all barriers.

George came over to help me and said, "What a great day!" I cheerfully agreed. With breakfast finished, Mike (with Lupe's help) asked who wanted to go to the laundromat. Just about every hand went up. To leave this room for a few hours would be a treat. Not that they couldn't, but that they had to sign in and out each time, even to smoke a cigarette, became a chore. We had two vans, Mike's and the van from Shelter 1, so 25 people could go. Mike suggested that several people wash and dry their clothes together. They agreed. People were asked to step forward who had money. About ten did. By asking many questions, Mike decided whose needs were greater and selected 15 others. He took me aside and gave me $40 to pay for those who couldn't. Money out of his own pocket! He truly cared for "his people."

I ended up with 10 men. Why, I don't know! The parking lot was unpaved, full of pot holes, and I think I hit every one. I heard snickering in back of me. Turning onto Route 9 South,

I took the turn too short and drove over the curb! Then I heard nervous laughter. Yes, I was a little embarrassed, even though this was my first time driving a van. I didn't know if anyone understood English but I said, "Fasten all seat belts!" Silence! We arrived safely and I parked where it was easy to park. We went into Sunbright Laundry, where I proceeded to show the men what clothes could be washed together along with how much soap, the setting, and how to operate the machine. Actually, I ended up doing it! Nancy (a volunteer) and I helped when needed, which was often.

Upon leaving, I found I had to back out onto busy Margaret Street. Great! How was I going to do that? From the back someone said something I did not understand. In the rear-view mirror I saw the men seated in the back, motioning to me to back up. I did and I was successful in getting underway. The whole van burst into cheers and clapping! I know one thing, men are the same the world over when it comes to women drivers. I smiled secretly.

Nancy left to return Shelter One's van for lunch and would not be back. That left Mike and me for lunch. Who would cover the phone? I suggested to Mike my next door neighbor, Barb Gilligan, might be able to help. He said, "Call her." I did, and with a little reassurance she agreed to come. While serving lunch she saw how little the refugees had for warm clothing. She left, and in late afternoon returned with her sons, Jimmy and Casey, carrying sweaters, warm socks and a few winter coats. Barb had gone home and cleaned out her closets!

Earlier in the afternoon there appeared a tall, white-haired, stately-looking man in a full dress blue uniform piped in red, an officer of the Salvation Army. Following him was a reporter and photographer from a Boston newspaper. Mike wasn't pleased to be interrupted by more reporters who took up his valuable time. Reporters from Canada, the Japanese media, Northeastern regions of New York, Vermont, Massachusetts, and New York City were just a few that had already been here. The refugee program at Plattsburgh would become an international story. A few minutes were spent with the reporter, and then Mike brought the Salvation Army Officer over, introducing him as the local Commander, Captain Jack Holcomb. I was impressed by this imposing, distinguished-looking man.

In walked Kathy Brandell Champagne, a young lady whose family lived not far from us. We had watched Kathy grow into a competitive runner through her high school years and her years at the University of New Hampshire. She was our local celebrity and still competed. I thought she was a new volunteer, but no, she was working with Social Services. She had been working on the refugee problem since December of last year and now she was out in the field.

My busy shift was about over around four o'clock, when Mike mentioned he wished there could be cookies or cupcakes for the people to eat in the evening. Everything edible was taken back to Shelter 1 each day since there was no refrigeration or proper storage area. I told Mike I would call the president of the Women's Club of Saint Mary's of the Lake, Cumberland Head, and see what could be done. "It would be nice of you, Fran, if you would." He looked so tired. Later that evening I called the president of the club, Irene Carter. She agreed to get in touch with her members.

The phone rang and I was greeted with a cheery "Hello, Mom, how are you?" It was Michael Ann, "Mike," my daughter-in-law from Colchester, Vermont. She asked me what I had been doing "to keep out of trouble." She did not know I had become involved in the refugee program. She was surprised, but supportive in my efforts and quite interested about the need for winter clothing in sizes ranging from adults to babies.

Later that night, while watching the 11 o'clock late news on WPTZ Channel 5, anchorwoman Erin Clark reported that Governor Cuomo had promised state aid. It was great news, for more refugees had arrived and Shelter Two truly had become undesirable living quarters. Ms. Clark went on to report that the plans worked on since January and early February by the directors of agencies and local political leaders would now be put into action. Construction had begun in the new 30,000 square foot Association for Retarded Citizens (ARC) building, located in the Industrial Park in the Town of Plattsburgh, with 12–hour shifts around the clock. (ARC had agreed to let their building be used as a refugee shelter on a temporary basis until they were ready to occupy it.) Channel 5 went on to report that the refugees from Shelters 1 and 2 would be moved into the main building on Sunday.

Well, John, you aren't going to see much of me this weekend, I silently thought. How was the new shelter going to be completed in time? How would it be possible to move so many? I was not "paid" to worry about such things, just to be there, and I was to report for 8:30 a.m. the following day.

Saturday, March 7

I was met at the door of the office by Mike. "You are going to the border with a young man this morning. Take my car and bring his girlfriend along, for she is upset. She can spend a little more time with him that way." I decided to take my car, making sure both had their papers. We left at 9:00 a.m., taking twenty minutes to get to the border. On the way, in the back seat I heard soft crying and quiet words that I did not understand. I tilted the rear view mirror, for I felt like an intruder. We arrived at the Canadian Immigration booth where I informed the officer I had two Guatemalan refugees with me. I told him the young man was entering for his hearing date but the young lady would be returning back with me. He told me to go to the Immigration Office, handing me a yellow card. I took them into a rather large room divided by a waist-high counter with four or five desks behind it, where seated officers were talking in French. A woman officer came over to the counter and greeted me with "Bon jour." I answered in English that I had brought a young man to enter for his hearing, but the young lady would be returning with me. I gave her the yellow card. She asked them for their papers, then told the young man to go through a door in the back and told us to wait. One hour passed and she had not returned to give the young lady her papers back. After another half hour, I approached the counter and asked where she was. Finally returning, she told me that the "young woman refugee has come back into Canada illegally." What does this mean?, I wondered. Do they impound my car? Hold me for illegal transportation? She told me her supervisor was redoing the lady's papers. Did this mean that she would get a new hearing date or a delay for her entry into Canada? The officer didn't know and disappeared again. God, I felt I had really fouled up! A half hour later she reappeared. She told me her supervisor had not changed the original hearing date, meaning the young woman could enter Canada on Monday. The officer returned the papers and emphasized to me not to do this again. "Ignorance of the law excuses no one." I assured her I would not!

I returned to the American border where the officer in the booth took the papers, put them in a cylinder and they disappeared. He told me to go into the Immigration Building. Here we go again! We went to the counter where I overheard an Immigration Officer telling another officer, "If you have a problem, just ask me."

I interjected, "Boy do I have a problem!" He came over with a smile on his face and asked what my problem was. I told him about the disappearing papers and hoped there would not be a problem with the young lady reentering the United

States. He found my rider's papers in the incoming box, returned still smiling, checked them quickly and gave them back to her. He said, "Have a good day." My day improved instantly with my heart once again beating properly. Three and a half hours had passed by the time we arrived back. Mike asked, "How come?" I told him and added, "Never again, Mike, do I take someone with me." He laughed.

After lunch a Clinton County Public Health nurse, Darlene Edwards, arrived for her very first time. A look of fear was on her face such as I had shown, I am sure, just a few days before. A small table with two chairs was set up in a corner with her meager supplies. Wearing a face mask and disposable gloves, she administered to those who were ill. She didn't look too comfortable when she informed Mike that one young man had pubic lice. His new blankets from his cot and the clothes he was wearing were to be bagged, and the man was to shower with medication before he could move tomorrow. The young man wasn't happy to give up his clothing, but was persuaded to do so as he was handed a set of clean clothing by Mike. Who was going to do the bagging? Not me! Mervin did, as he was on duty that afternoon.

New York State Social Service Commissioner Cesar A. Perales was the main lead-in story for Erin Clark on the Channel 5 evening news. He had come to meet today with local officials and brought a check with him for $177,000 from the State of New York, dated March 5, 1987. Other state assistance, $60,000, was being made available from emergency funds to complete the new shelter.

The financial structure was already in place. It had been set up earlier by Tom Schmitz, from Divisional Headquarters of the Salvation Army located in Syracuse, New York. The ordering of supplies would be done by Ginger Spies, secretary of the local Salvation Army, from Plattsburgh Grocery, Buck Paper, Bouyea Bakery and Flickingers wholesale grocery in

Syracuse. The set of financial books for the Department of Social Services "refugee fund," for supplies and their payment, would be kept by Nancy Tyrell, bookkeeper at the local Salvation Army. The "Nursing Disaster Plan" of the American Red Cross had been set up and put in place at the main shelter by director Jeanie Roberts. The plan was to be implemented by the Public Health nurses from and under the supervision of Nancy Smith of the Clinton County Health Department. Thus this shelter and refugee relief program would be different than others, where churches are often the mainstay.

Unexpectedly, a car pulled into our driveway around 7:00 that evening. It was Mike, my daughter-in-law from Vermont, with her station wagon stuffed with several thirty-gallon sized bags of clothing! She had got on the phone after speaking with me and called all her friends. They went through their closets, gathering hats, winter coats, gloves, and more importantly, children's winter clothing in sizes for babies up to toddlers. Then Mike collected all the items and took the Lake Champlain Ferry to bring it all to Plattsburgh.

We drove to Shelter 2 with the clothing and within ten minutes everything was gone! Mike is originally from Albuquerque, New Mexico, where Spanish is prevalently spoken. She was able to speak a few words in Spanish with the happy mothers as they went through the baby clothes. We talked non-stop all the way home of the joy brought by her donations to those in such dire need. After a quick cup of coffee she left for the return trip home.

I was proud of my daughter-in-law. I had seen a side of Mike I had not been completely aware of before. She showed concern for these people and a deep caring by making this trip alone at night.

Sunday, March 8

When I arrived mid-morning I saw the 962nd Ordinance Corps of the Army Reserve, along with the Salvation Army, loading refugee possessions into their trucks. Church buses were loaded with refugees. The move was already under way. I found Mike. He sent me into the housing area to find a young lady named Maggie who was translating. If she needed me I was to stay. If not, I was to go back to the office to answer phones.

I saw a young man with a cast on his leg using crutches. He stood next to a small, delicate young woman who was calling out names and directing them to line up near the door to be transported to the new shelter. I introduced myself to the man and learned his name was Kevin Talcott. He was with the Air Force stationed here in Plattsburgh. Maggie (Maria Fernandez-Talcott), his wife, was American-Cuban and fluent in Spanish. She had responded to the desperate call for translators. I met their little boy Michael, who was playing with the other children, unfazed by all the commotion. Everything was going smoothly in her capable hands so I returned to the office.

Incoming calls from Shelter 1 would give the OK when our next bus load of refugees was to leave from here. The trips were alternated, first Shelter 1, then Shelter 2, so everyone did not arrive all at once at the new location. With seemingly flawless communications and teamwork the transfer was made with no problems. Just as the last bus left, in drove Betty Daly and Rita Richards, delivering several dozen cupcakes and cookies which had been made by the Women's Club of Saint Mary's of The Lake. Since we were in the process of moving, they went out of their way and followed me to the "Main Shelter." This small but active club showed its compassion and generosity by baking "goodies" for grateful refugees.

What a large building! The workmen had converted an empty 30,000 square foot building, dividing it into two.

The first 15,000 square feet were living quarters. The other side was to be used for storage of cots, blankets, suitcases, baby cribs and boxes of winter clothing. The clothing was sized by boxes for men, boys, women, children and babies. There were also boxes of boots, shoes, winter hats and gloves. The building was self-contained, except for cooking facilities, which would continue at the Salvation Army building with the prepared food being transported to the shelter. I brought the "goodies" to the dining area. It was huge, with four rows of four tables per row with chairs where 150 to 180 people could be seated and fed at one time. Bags and suitcases, which had been transported by trucks from Shelter 1 and 2, were piled high in one part of the dining area where refugees who had completed the initial processing were claiming their belongings with the help of a translator.

The move from Shelter 1 and 2 was thus completed. There were reporters everywhere. I went to see where I could help and was told to report to what would become known as the "game room." Refugees were being processed, having their pictures taken for personal ID cards. This never worked out and was dropped in coming weeks. I was asked to show those processed to their assigned living quarters.

The living quarters were set up so that single men were together in one section, single women in another section, and families in another separate section. Families from the same culture enjoyed being next to one other, for the sharing and visiting made time pass more quickly.

Before my day was done, I found the "Emergency Salvation Army Shelter," as it was named, had 38 ten-by-sixteen sheetrock cubicles with four cots, blankets and pillows per unit. The blankets and cots had been provided not only by the local American Red Cross and the National Guard, but also its units from Essex, Franklin and other surrounding counties in New York, as well as from the State of Vermont. The pillows were provided by the State University at Plattsburgh. The shelter was soon filled with 150 refugees from the two original shelters. The ceiling was open, with huge heating units hanging from girders, glaring bright lights, and the outside walls were made of sheet metal. The dining area had windows across the entire front letting sunlight fill the room.

More important, the refugees now had a small amount of privacy and comfort. Their faces reflected joy as they stored their few belongings and chatted happily in their native tongue. Children of all cultures played together in a special carpeted play area.

Every agency was on hand to provide its particular service and help the refugees settle in. Working together, they organized a smoothly run operation.

This "Emergency Shelter" had a complete infirmary, installed plumbing for laundry, two rooms of three showers each, four bathrooms with two toilets and two sinks per unit. There was a public phone for refugee use, out-calling only, in the dining area. In the main office there were three phones for incoming and outgoing calls, and a phone for Social Services representatives. All operated on an intercommunication system and had been installed and completed by New York Telephone Company the previous Friday.

Arby's, Wendy's and Kentucky Fried Chicken brought food in to feed the hungry refugees. There had been no time today to cook at or transport from the Salvation Army kitchen.

For the first time Barb Gilligan and I met our supervisor, the new coordinator of volunteers at Catholic Charities, Margot Zeglis. A striking, fashionable blonde lady with the most beautiful smile, she asked if I could come tomorrow for 8:00 a.m., and she would also see me at that time to set hours I could work. Volunteers were still desperately needed. It was the beginning of a warm relationship between Margot and me. She would become a friend, a patron and mentor to me.

I was home by 5:30 p.m. What a day!

Monday, March 9

The next morning I pulled into the nearly empty paved parking lot at the Emergency Shelter. As I walked down the sidewalk and passed in front of the large windows of the dining area, I saw many refugees eating a breakfast of dough-nuts, donated by Dunkin Donuts and Rambach's Bakery, and drinking coffee. I entered the door to the main office where a desk was manned by Bob Davies, who had been on night duty. The desk held a large log book where everyone—staff, vol-unteers, visitors and refugees—would provide the following requested information: your name, time in/out, where you were going if leaving the building and why. The main office was quite comfortable, with a carpeted floor and large TV which refugees could use. The Salvation Army had hung their "Emergency Shelter" sign in the front window near the entrance door. The American flag, and the Salvation Army, flag with their shield, "Blood and Fire," were on display near the window. Bob handed me sheets of paper with the policy and rules of the Salvation Army operation of this shelter. To my left were three desks where two volunteers were answer-ing incoming calls, recording time, the callers' names, and the messages. With just enough room to squeeze around the last volunteer's desk, there were two more desks located next to the door that entered into the large dining area. These desks were used by Kathy Champagne and Maureen Lynch from Social Services. It was here they would meet, process and assign rooms to new arrivals or meet with refugees who had problems or questions. (I would go to Kathy more than once with problems that surfaced at the shelter. Working under her guidance and Maureen's, I was aware of and greatly admired their gentleness and their compassion shown to the frightened refugees.)

One of the many duties Kathy and Maureen had was to process medical vouchers for sick refugees who had to go to the doctor, the hospital, or to the pharmacy to have a prescription filled. A volunteer had to have a medical voucher in hand before transporting the sick refugee for medical treatment or to fill a prescription. Kathy and Maureen also had at their station the complete list of names of refugees and where they were housed in the shelter with their assigned dates of entry into Canada, as well as a list of professor's names from SUNY at Plattsburgh as translators for Middle Eastern and Eastern languages (Arabic, Persian, Armenian). The evening/night supervisor and his staff had access to all the forms in the desks for use with new refugees arriving after 5:00 p.m.

Bob Davies took me on a tour of the shelter. In the dining area was a small locked storage room which held the cleaning products, sponges, throw-away gloves, large mops, brooms, garbage bags and disinfectants needed to maintain the shelter. Located also in the dining area was a Coca-Cola vending machine, four washers and four dryers. In the back "Exit" area, which had an alarm system that would sound in the "Main Office" if the door was opened, was a fairly large carpeted children's play area with toys. In the far northwest corner was a large storage area kept locked that held dried food, cases of juice, bars of soap, shampoo, face cloths, towels, toothbrushes, toothpaste, razors, shaving cream, men's and women's American Red Cross "kits," paper products for meals, plastic spoons, knives and forks, cups, Pampers of all sizes and many personal items. Everything was supplied that a person would need! These storage areas were inspected and approved by the Public Health Department every two weeks. The keys for these areas were always kept in the front desk that was manned by a Salvation Army Officer or a member of that organization.

Upon our return Bob introduced me to Salvation Army Captain David Champlin who had just arrived for the day shift. He was from Troy, New York, and would be here only temporarily until a permanent officer could be assigned. He seemed very nice, with a casual attitude evidenced by his removal of the jacket of his dress uniform.

Lloyd Mori was the night supervisor for the Crisis Center. He oversaw three or four Plattsburgh State students who were working for that agency. After having taken a leave of absence from his studies, Lloyd was a returning student in his senior year working towards a BA degree. We seemed to hit it off instantly, developing a friendly relationship. Lloyd had a very difficult time getting around to completing "boring" paperwork, whether for refugees or doing college term papers, but somehow he always came through. Paperwork was just not Lloyd's cup of tea.

The shelter was manned 24 hours a day with staff foot-patrols every 20 minutes, inside and outside, during the night. The night shift consisted of staff from the Crisis Center and a disaster team member from Salvation Army. The day shift consisted of an officer or member of the Salvation Army, volunteers, Social Services employees and a nurse.

Bob Davies asked me to give him a ride home. It had been a long night. Lloyd said he would see me later, he had a college paper to finish before class that afternoon.

Upon my return the shelter was buzzing with activity. Children were exploring every nook of their new home. People were washing and drying clothes. Lupe and other interpreters, including Maggie, were busy translating from English to Spanish the rules and signs in the dining room. These would be posted throughout the building. Duties for cleaning were being drawn up. Names selected from the list of refugees would be posted for cleaning bathrooms and showers, mopping floors and emptying trash. The list usually consisted of five men and five women to be assigned for one week. This was also true for cooking meals. Assisting the cook would be up to, but no more than, eight people. The cook in charge stayed until he left for Canada, which could be up to four weeks. Depending upon the population at any given time, it could be two weeks or more before someone drew duty again. It was important that the refugees themselves maintain the shelter in all aspects.

It was surprising how many refugees offered to help. Many were chosen for their ability to command respect from the other refugees. They were asked to take a "supervisory" position to keep track of who had worked and who had not. They were to make up charts with names of those who had not worked and post them in the dining area with assigned duties. It was also the supervisory refugee's responsibility to see that the crew for cooking was ready to leave on time in the morning, and that the cleaning of the shelter was properly done. This task required a special person that the refugees respected, for many would feel he was "brown-nosing the Gringos" and think he was better than them by holding such a position.

The cleaning crew began shortly after 9 a.m. and the cooking crew left at this time to prepare lunch. I took the Salvation Army van to transport the cooking crew and returned. Someone would go at 11:30 a.m. to bring them and the meal back. Lunch was to be served by 12:30 p.m.

Barb arrived after her boys had left for school and I would see her often throughout the busy day. Barb transported the sick to the doctor where she would stay with them and then stop at Meyer's Pharmacy to fill a prescription if needed, as Meyer's had agreed to accept medical vouchers from the Department of Social Services. On this day Barb left with the van to pick up the crew and lunch. Lunch was delicious! Homemade vegetable soup in a tomato base, rice with pieces of chicken that was a little hot on the tongue, bread, boxes of bananas, and Kool-Aid. The cooking crew would return around 1:30 p.m. to the Salvation Army building to start working on dinner. All cooking supplies and food were delivered and kept at the Salvation Army building where a refrigerated trailer held the perishable food. Everything was kept locked, including the large storage room holding said supplies. The crew had to make sure the kitchen was "spic and span" before they left for the day. More refugees offered to work cooking duty, for they could then prepare breakfast of eggs and toast for themselves before starting lunch.

After lunch the storage room holding cleaning supplies was unlocked by a volunteer or a staff member for the cleaning crew to sweep/mop the dining area. This was done after breakfast and again after lunch. The halls were also swept and mopped each day. It was work and the majority did it without complaint. However, the young men of all cultures seemed to get a lot of "headaches" or claimed not to "feel well."

I answered telephones after lunch that seemed to ring constantly even though two other volunteers were answering as well. Ginger, from the Salvation Army building, called to inform me that community people were on their way with toys, books, clothing and another portable TV. In addition, Peryea's of West Chazy, a local business, would be loaning and setting up satellite dishes within the next two days. Now Spanish programs could be received and seen by the refugees. Ginger also said that Valley Vending would be bringing video game machines later in the day. Many local businesses would donate, loan or give their services. I was proud of my city and its residents in their response to a happening that was so far from the norm. I asked Captain Champlin where all these things were going to be placed. Surely not in the "main office." "No, we have an empty room which will be turned into a game room," he replied. Good, I thought . . . we sure didn't need to have noisy game machines along with non-stop ringing phones!

"Hi, this is Bob Robare from the Town of Plattsburgh," said the voice on the other end of the next call I answered. (I knew Bob; he was the youth coordinator for the town of Plattsburgh.) He told me he had an extra ping-pong table with a set of paddles that he would be delivering this afternoon. He would be bringing weight-lifting equipment later in the week. When Bob arrived he approached Captain Champlin about an idea. He suggested setting up basketball teams made up of young refugee men. He would then arrange with Saint Alexander's School, located in Morrisonville, to allow the refugees to play basketball several nights a week in their gym. He would be willing to teach and supervise. Captain Champlin thought it was a great idea. The school was just a few miles from the shelter and transportation would not be a problem. We had just received two vans rented by the Department of Social Services (out of the monies from the "refugees fund") under a lease agreement with E.S. Mason, Inc., a Plattsburgh car-leasing company.

I did not go home for dinner. There was a shortage of volunteers; John understood. My day ended at 10:00 p.m. when the night shift came on duty. I was to come in at 10:00 a.m. tomorrow. I left tired. It had been a fourteen hour day of excitement. What would tomorrow bring? I looked forward to it!

Tuesday, March 10

I saw lovely Margot today or I should say she found me. We spoke at length about what hours I could give. There still were not enough volunteers to do what needed to be done. However, people were coming forward even if only to offer a few hours. Volunteers were needed to cover from 6:00 or 7:00 a.m. until 10:00 p.m. The infamous phones needed to be answered. Refugees needed transportation to the Salvation Army store for two complete sets of clothing, a winter coat, and boots or shoes. Transportation was needed for the sick, for those needing prescriptions, for the cooking crew, and for going for last-minute needed items at local stores or the Salvation Army building. I told her I could come anytime and stay as long as needed at this time. She was surprised and pleased as she scheduled me for this day until 2:00 p.m. For the rest of the week, including Sunday, she scheduled a time for me to come in, but left the end of the shift open to my own discretion.

The following is an example of a schedule:

Wed. & Thurs.	6:00 a.m. - 4:00 p.m.
Friday	10:00 a.m. - 8:30 p.m.
Saturday	7:00 a.m. - 6:00 p.m.
Sunday	6:00 p.m. - 10:00 p.m.

In weeks to come I would start at 6:00 a.m. or 7:00 a.m. Margot posted the schedule with the volunteers' telephone numbers directly behind the volunteers' desk on the wall. Staff could see who should be on, and if they were late would call another volunteer to come in.

The staff was meeting with refugees in the dining area to set up its own "manned patrols," two men on, two-hour shifts, with flashlights provided by the Salvation Army. Their shifts would encompass the time period from 10:00 p.m. to 7:00 a.m. Refugee men stepped forward to volunteer with one chosen by them to set up the schedule and be their leader. These patrols proved to work out very well. They were now policing themselves instead of being policed by the "Gringos." If a problem arose it usually was settled by the men; if not, the night staff was called in. The policy of the shelter was, if need be, call the sheriff. To my knowledge this occurred several times but the incidents were settled amicably.

A day/night logbook was kept by staff members. The night shift would make an entry to draw attention to a problem, such as "need to see the nurse." The day shift would enter anything that the night shift should be aware of. At times it was very interesting to read. Most of the time it was routine.

For the evening staff coming on duty, an entry appeared asking a staff member to look in on a young lady named Noemi whom I had taken to the Emergency Room at the Champlain Valley Physicians Hospital Medical Center (CVPH). (I will use only first names for reasons of confidentialty. I will also tell, when possible, the refugee's reason for leaving their country.) Noemi began having acute pain in her stomach just after Alice Farbotko, assigned "refugee nurse," had left. I called John to let him know I would be late again tonight. No problem; he understood. I took Noemi and a friend of hers who spoke English to the emergency room where she was admitted to a small curtained-off room. Standing next to her as she laid on the cold table with just a sheet covering her, I took her hand in mine. Her eyes were filled with fright and glistening with tears as she grasped my hand tightly. In a soft, gentle voice I spoke reassuring words as her friend translated. For an instant a smile played on her lips, our eyes communicating where no words were spoken. A dinner tray was brought in for Noemi; she couldn't eat, so her friend did.

When the doctor had finished his examination he took me outside and told me he felt her stomach was very irritated from not eating properly, along with stress and worry. He said she should eat light foods, crackers, toast, etc., in small amounts, but often, and to drink milk. He wrote down his diagnosis to be taken back by me for the nurse. He would give her some medication that would help.

Noemi became like my child. I would check in on her several times a day in her cubicle. Though we didn't speak one another's language, she understood my concern for her. Through my improvised sign language she understood when I asked if she had eaten. Milk and crackers were now unlimited to her. Every morning I would go to her and my last act before going home was to see her and bid her "buenos noches," good-night. The shelter was still settling in and buzzing with activity as I went out into the night.

The shelter had become a living thing! Pulsating, maintaining, rejuvenating itself, and unto itself holding hundreds of stories, each unique, yet the same. The flight to freedom!

Thursday, March 12

Today would be a special day for the shelter and her people, for New York State Governor Mario Cuomo was making a visit. I quote the following, a part of his statement:

> The people who deserve the congratulations are . . . all the people of Clinton County, all the people of Plattsburgh, who have the whole state very, very proud. The refugees felt your love in Plattsburgh. There's no force in the whole world as great as that; there's no bayonets, no guns, nothing as strong as that.

Saturday, March 14

I was met by Lloyd as the night shift was going off, and told to go immediately to the maternity ward at the hospital to relieve Ed, a night-staff member. (A pregnant woman, Fatima, had been brought there shortly after her arrival last evening.) Lloyd told me to stay until the doctor had seen "the mother to-be," and if she was released to return her and her husband to the shelter. If not, I was to report to the nurse at the shelter who would be in by 9:00 a.m.

I relieved Ed, a night-staff member, who looked exhausted. After getting names from him, he quickly left to get much-needed sleep. Fatima, who was three months pregnant, did not look very well. I walked in with a smile, receiving a weak smile in return. Her husband, who spoke English, was quite concerned. After being examined by a doctor, it was decided she should stay the day and be watched. Gus, her husband, would stay with her. Again, it was a story of too much stress and traveling for days from El Salvador. Most of the refugees took the long bus ride from New York City to the border, spending many hours there, then returning to the shelter in Plattsburgh without having eaten properly and in a state of exhaustion. There would be many occurrences such as these. They experienced fright and the unknown in a world they did not understand.

Reporters and photographers were still coming even though press releases were being given each day at the Government Center by Commissioner Rose Pandozy and Captain Holcomb. They searched for the one story not told or the one picture that would tell more than " a thousand words." Many refugees refused to speak or have their picture taken because of family left behind. They were afraid of reprisals to their loved ones if a picture or story was read or seen by their government officials.

Tuesday, March 17

Today I made a border run to take refugees by van for their entry into Canada. I was asked by Captain Champlin would if it be OK for reporter Enrique Corredera to ride in the van to the border. He wanted to interview a family from Guatemala, follow them through their hearing in Montréal and the process a refugee goes through once in Canada. A car with photographer, Mark Sasahara, followed me. Both were from the *Burlington* [VT] *Free Press*.

Though the interview was in Spanish, I will take excerpts from his article which appeared in a later issue:

The father of two is an electrical engineer and the son of an elementary school teacher. In his interview he stated that in

41

his country to be educated and to be respected in society is a crime. "All who are studying have problems with the military government because they can't be manipulated easily.

"If you write an article that the government doesn't like, you disappear. If relatives ask about your whereabouts, they tell them you were part of the subversion and have left for Cuba.

"It would be nice if they fired a shot, you wouldn't feel anything, but they cut in pieces first."

As he stared out the window of the green, rusty van his wife added: "Do you know what my greatest fear was? They are known to abuse your children while they tie up your husband to watch, then they kill him." For a month the family lived out of suitcases in motels and shelters in Plattsburgh. Their journey of 108 days and 6,000 miles had included a nighttime crossing into the United States from Mexico with the help of a paid "coyote" guide. (Coyotes were men paid to smuggle illegal people across the border into the United States.)

There were brief stays in San Diego, Los Angeles and New York and finally the abortive bus trip and rejection at the Canadian border last month.

This is just one of many political persecutions that I heard. It was this way in many cultures and countries around the world. Not only did the educated leave, but many of the poor arrived with just the clothes on their back. They were caught between military governments and guerrilla forces. Especially if you were a young man of 14 years or older and living in guerrilla controlled areas, you would be forced to join. If you didn't, then you were with the government forces. You and family members, in many cases, could be killed.

One night at the shelter, a newly arrived Central American man was found pacing, facing the wall, back and forth, the length of what would be a prison cell. When examined by the nurse she found he had been tortured with cigarette burns all over his body. He was taken to the CVPH Medical Center and then transferred to a facility for intensive mental treatment. Several months later, on medication, he was released and allowed to enter Canada. Canada had agreed to delay his hearing date while he was in treatment. And so it went, seeing the mental and physical abuse passing our way.

The hours are like minutes with my days passing quickly, almost in a blur. The shelter is becoming my second home, a demanding child to whom I happily give my "mothering."

Spring, 1987

Tuesday, March 24

Darlene had now replaced Alice, the original refugee nurse, who had been assigned since February. Alice had "burned out" and had asked to go back to regular public nursing. Since Darlene had covered on weekends, she got the assignment. She would work Monday through Friday, 9 a.m. to 5 p.m. in the infirmary. I could understand the "burnout" with so many health screenings and ministering to the sick.

Darlene loved her work and these people. She met former doctors who assisted her, but did not diagnose or prescribe. From these doctors Darlene learned about their lives, conditions and medical treatment in their country. Her compassion for the young and old went beyond her job. Often she would drop in evenings after work or on weekends, bringing needed items like over-the-counter drugs, to talk, just to see how things were going.

When the five members of the first "security patrol" were to leave for Canada, she bought T-shirts for each. She then hand-painted the following inscription with the motto that is represented on the Salvation Army flag, adding her "pet" name for them:

Blood and Fire
Salvation Army
Night Hawks

They loved them.

She found cases, either because of a lack of knowledge or lack of medical treatment in their countries, that were life-threatening medical problems, such as the woman suffering from advanced pneumonia for three weeks who did not receive medical attention until reaching Plattsburgh, and even then she didn't ask for treatment. It was found only during her health screen, which all refugees received upon their arrival. Another sat through hours of interviews and paperwork before making her problem known to Darlene. She pointed to her body and tried to indicate that something had to be cleansed. Darlene realized she was pointing to her kidneys and would need dialysis treatment.

Jose Madan, who came to the United States from Cuba in 1955, owns and operates Madan Laboratory. He instructed his laboratory to do any tests Darlene deemed necessary without charge.

At daily meetings immediate staff members were made aware of the need to address all health problems, especially with the increase in the refugee population. Therefore, meetings with videos and explanations were made available to all refugees on a regular basis. They were given by the nurse and a staff member from Social Services in conjunction with another immediate staff member of the shelter.

Saturday, March 28

My turn came to be with the crew for preparing lunch on Saturday, leaving at 9 a.m. I had heard how other volunteers found this to be the least-liked duty for them. However, we alternated and I soon found out why—boring, boring, boring!

The main building that held the kitchen facilities was closed weekends. That meant I had to go to Captain Holcomb's home located nearby to pick up (and return) keys to unlock the building, storage rooms and the refrigerated trailer. I was to accompany the crew while they got supplies to make sure nothing, but nothing, was taken except what was necessary to prepare the meal. The volunteer was answerable directly to Captain Holcomb. As the cooking crew prepared the meal they would sometimes sing or just chat in their native tongue. I would read or, to their delight, attempt to shoot basketball hoops. The crew was very well organized, with the chief cook shouting out orders. My preparation of home meals should go so well. We left by 12:00 noon for the shelter, and I never failed in hitting a dip when entering the South Catherine Street Bridge, causing cases of bread to fly onto the floor and spilling soup in the van. You could smell the soup in the van for a week. I think this happened to every driver. I was happy, though, to draw this duty only occasionally. I preferred to be where the action was at the shelter.

Upon my return I found a new policy was handed down by Captain Holcomb. All packages were to be inspected at the manned desk by the door. Apparently alcoholic beverages were coming into the shelter.

Monday, March 30

Barb was in everyday, going home as before to pick Jimmy and Casey up and returning to run errands with the van, taking her sons with her. She had become one of the most dedicated volunteers in the program.

Late this afternoon she and her boys walked in with bags of basketball-type socks. She had bought K-Mart out, taking every size they had. "When you see barefoot children, women and men you don't give a second thought," she said. Jim, her husband, said to me, "Fran, you introduced Barb to the

45

program and that is the last I saw of her." Not quite true Jim, but darn close. She took on the W.I.C. program, a Federal program allowing extra food for pregnant women and for children up to four years of age. She spent a lot of time on this program, using her car at her own expense, in addition to many hours at the shelter.

Such was the case with Sue Steuart and husband Bernie, owners of Dairy Queen. Sue contacted Ron Wood of Wood's Floor Covering and told him of the cold cement floor that children, women and men stepped on each morning. Within two days Ron and his men were at the shelter to cut and lay remnants of carpet in the cubicles. Again another business-man responding to a need, but Ron would return to the shelter and also give of himself with his music.

Sue did not stop there! If items were needed that we could not obtain from supplies at the Salvation Army, she would buy them: crackers, juice and more Pampers for babies or young children. The need was there; she responded with no questions. "You just do it," she said.

Fifteen to thirty refugees were leaving per day, and just as many were arriving. Sue would come in the evening with supplies for sandwiches, an assortment of fruits, and beverages. She prepared a bag for each person about to leave, with their name on it, to be handed out by staff in the morning. A refrigerator was now in the main office to keep medication for the sick or special foods. Now it also held the little bags that were gratefully taken by those leaving on the day of their entry. Refugees could wait up to eight hours at the Canadian Border before they left for Montréal and there wasn't anything for them to buy to eat.

Sue would walk with frightened refugees around the large living quarters or sit and listen to the outpouring of their pain. A volunteer doing "God's work" with love. Quietly living her belief without fanfare. Someone they could talk to, someone who listened, someone who did not turn away.

Tuesday, March 31

Donations of money in small amounts continued to come in from all parts of the country. However, there was always a shortage for the little extras not available from the "main fund."

A California-based Latin-American band named "Sabia," was to appear in Burlington, Vermont. When they heard about the refugees in Plattsburgh they quickly agreed to appear at Plattsburgh State University for a special performance and donated the proceeds to the refugee program. Again our local media got the word out on short notice with the community responding, making the evening quite successful.

Tuesday, April 7

Captain Champlin has been replaced by another officer, Captain Suarez from Rochester.

In the two short weeks that Captain Champlin was here he neither looked nor acted as stern as Captain Holcomb. He would sit and eat with the refugees and try his few words of Spanish on them. They would laugh with glee . . . and so would he. When he had to leave he did so with regret, for he had become attached to the shelter and what it represented—a way station to freedom.

Captain Suarez only stayed two weeks, but since he spoke Spanish he was able to communicate directly to the majority of refugees at the shelter. Then came Lt. Judy Potter from Buffalo. I found myself working with her and being drawn more and more into this place of refuge, the living quarters. I would drive if needed, but more volunteers were coming forward so I turned to the heart—the people.

Paul Cote and I were the first day shift volunteers to arrive at 6 or 7 a.m. Paul had such a great sense of humor. We would go outside with Lloyd and have our coffee while the night staff cleaned the main office. Paul's and Lloyd's tall tales always made my day start with a smile.

Either Paul or I would go to pick up Lt. Judy at 8:30 a.m. She and I would walk around the living quarters seeing what needed to be done, greeting the people and stopping for her to answer any questions that refugees might have. I soon was looking forward to greeting, talking and working with the refugees each day. I was exposed to customs I had only read about or seen in the media. Now, I was experiencing and learning first hand, taking advantage of each opportunity.

Wednesday, April 8

I had heard about the arrival of a young Sri Lankan girl of 16, under the care of an elderly chaperon. She stayed in her cubicle with her chaperon bringing her meals. She was on her way to Canada to marry a Sri Lanka man she had never met. It was an arranged marriage between families. When I saw her I found her appearance stunning. Her complexion was a glowing copper, her eyes were as black as ebony, and a long single braid of jet-black hair reached to her delicate waist. A red dot graced the center of her forehead. Her smart but simple attire was of the West. Always chaperoned, her manners spoke of inborn class, perhaps of nobility, and yet she was entering as a refugee in order to marry.

Sri Lankan women, with drawn high collars on their long flowing, colorful dresses, cannot quite conceal their heavy gold necklaces. Yet, for the few that had financial means, there were so many more that had so little or nothing at all.

The women of Sri Lanka, as in many other cultures, are submissive to men. There is also a caste system in this culture. Women carry suitcases or packages, with men walking nearly empty-handed a few paces ahead. I came face to face with this one day.

One van or the other always seemed to be in the garage for repairs so it meant the use of private cars when this happened. I was to pick up a prescription at the pharmacy and I was asked by a former professor from Sri Lanka to take him to the mall so he could exchange an item. It was fine, I would be going by the mall anyway and I thought he would walk back. Word went out and I soon had four Central American women who wanted to go, one being Noemi who was now much better.

On arriving at the mall, I opened the trunk for him to get his item, he pointed to one woman to fetch his item. He turned to me and said, "You will pick me up on your return trip." He didn't ask, it was an order expected to be followed. I informed him I could not do this, nor would the woman carry his item, as she was about to do. I told him he must carry his own parcel, adding that it was a nice day for a walk. Yet I knew, and tried to understand, this was normal in his culture. He was apologetic and took his item. He no longer demanded, as he had done in the past to volunteers, but instead would say, "If not out of your way," showing respect to us. A few others that came were like him, but hundreds were not and helped us in any way they could. They cleaned, even if not very quickly, sometimes taking three hours to do a bathroom. They took their turn without complaint.

In Somalia, which is in the eastern part of Africa, the culture is much the same. Men look down on women. Discrimination against women is embedded in the culture and the religion. However, I never had occasion where this came into play. There was an occasion, however, where a young man did not want to get up for his cleaning duties; women do the cleaning. The supervisor, who was Central American, could not get him up to work. I went to his cubicle and asked him, "Why?" He said he "had a headache." I replied, "I do too," and to my own surprise, found myself pulling the blanket off him! He was wearing long pants, but still I was shocked at myself that I had done this. With afterthought, it reminded me of when my sons were young and they didn't feel like getting up. I asked him to be out in five minutes to start cleaning. Lo and behold, he was.

Friday, April 10

Many refugees became like family to many Plattsburgh volunteers. They were often invited to a volunteer's home for dinner or just for an evening away from the shelter. Relationships developed that led to meaningful friendships.

Barb, with her seven year old son Casey, was transporting Rosa, who was eight-and-a-half months pregnant, and Rosa's husband Alfredo to the doctor. To Barb's total embarrassment, Casey asked, "Why are you here?" Alfredo answered Casey, "My father was shot and killed in our front yard in front of me. I do not know why or who did it." From that day on, until Alfredo and Rosa left for Canada, a special bond existed between them and Casey. Whenever Casey was with his mother at the shelter he would go and seek them out while Jimmy went to find his friend from Lebanon.

Jimmy, Barb's oldest son, had met George, which led to a close relationship with many happy hours spent together. When George left for Montréal he gave Jimmy his guitar. Alfredo gave a "Capirucho" to Casey, a hand-held Central American game. The day that Rosa and Alfredo were at the border for their entry, Rosa went into labor—two weeks early. An ambulance transported them to a Montréal hospital where they became parents to a little girl whom they named Casey. This is the volunteer's reward, the making of very special friendships that knows no barriers.

Saturday, April 11

Rosemary McNamara walked in one day and asked me, "What can I do? Where do you need me?" I took her on a tour and by the time we returned to the main office I found out that this young lady was on the Board of Directors of the American Red Cross, a trustee of her church, active in community services, and married to Bob, who was in the Air Force. She had two boys, Ben and Colin, and took great interest in their sporting events. Where would she find time to volunteer? Somehow she did and we became close friends. Why? I don't know. I was old enough to be her mother (well, almost). Rosemary came in for two to three hours per day until she took a job with the American Red Cross as their representative on the Air Base. Like most other volunteers, she and I made close friends with some of the refugees, especially Oscar from El Salvador.

Oscar from El Salvador writing work crew schedules.
Emergency Salvation Army Shelter,
Town of Plattsburgh, 1987.

Oscar had arrived the end of March and offered on the night of his arrival to help in any way. He was a distinguished-looking man in his early forties and held a Master's degree from Michigan State. Through his and his family's efforts he had been a successful businessman in his country.

Then came the day, in front of his family and in his home, when armed soldiers burst in and took him away. His family did not know where he had been taken. They checked all police stations, but were told he wasn't there. They were about to make an appeal to the Bishop of the Catholic Church when he was released. He said he was picked up with twenty other men, questioned and released after 12 days. To this day he doesn't know why. He surmised that the government thought he knew people in the rebel forces. He would always be a suspect so he left. He hoped his wife and three daughters would follow in May. Before they could come their personal affairs would have to be settled.

There was a need for a supervisor to make up lists of names of work crews and post them. Oscar's personality and character made him the right person for this difficult task. He accepted, and did wonderful work with no major problems. He was fair but firm, but more importantly the other refugees respected him.

Sunday, April 12

Lupe left today for her hearing date in Montréal, leaving the following "thank you" posted in the office:

> I couldn't express my gratitude not even with 1000 words. When we came from the Canadian border, we didn't know what to do, we were confused, and there was you.
> With love and care, you showed us the joy of sharing. People like you make the difference in this world. If I was to live my life again, I will live this experience all over again.
> I will remember you always.
>
> Lupe

Religious services were now being given for the refugees each week. Father Roger Martin, Catholic Pastor at nearby Dannemora, held a Spanish-language Mass each Thursday with Elaine Rodriguez of Plattsburgh organizing the Spanish liturgies. These services and the Protestant services, which were held on Sunday, took place in an empty classroom.

A special Mass for the Central Americans had been held in March at Saint Alexander's Church in Morrisonville and celebrated by Bishop Stanislaus J. Brzana of the Diocese of Odgensburg. Captain and Mrs. Jack Holcomb were in attendance as were many local priests, volunteers and guests. It was a moving celebration, with George from Lebanon playing his guitar and the Central Americans singing in their native language. They had practiced together for over a week. Two completely different cultures from opposite corners of the world joined together in their celebration and their music.

Following Mass the Knights of Columbus provided a brunch in the Parish Hall. The Bishop visited with everyone and took time to bless and welcome these despairing people. For a moment in their desperate lives they were free from fear and felt the arms of love.

Father Martin became more than the priest that came every Thursday to say Mass. He took more than twenty single young men over a period of time to live with him. Many had troubling problems, but came to look upon this gentle yet firm man as their father. He brought clothes, shoes, boots for them, and often went to Montréal to see how they were doing.

Tuesday, April 14

The shelter was not just a routine of filling paper dispensers, unlocking storage areas, getting breakfast supplies or getting crews underway. Each day held something different. This day the "Kitchen Band," under the direction of Josephine Speare, would come after lunch to entertain. The band, made up of retired men and women, were known throughout the Plattsburgh area for entertaining in nursing homes, the hospital and schools. Today they would be here to play before an international group who never before saw such a show. Arrangements were made by the Plattsburgh Interfaith Council (PIC). PIC is made up of interdenominational representatives from area churches. PIC arranged for French/English classes and paralegal assistance to be given in the shelter, entertainment and dances, Catholic and Protestant services, art classes, day care at the Methodist Church on Beekman Street, and schooling for the older children at Saint Alexander's school in Morrisonville. These are a few of the PIC activities or programs that I am aware of.

A gathering of a hundred or more waited patiently looking forward to the arrival of the Kitchen Band. There was no language barrier once they started to play, only smiles and laughter were seen and heard! Pedro (the "news star," as he was known, for all reporters sought him out) got up to dance by himself in his Central American step. Well, I could not let this pass! I joined him and gave him a quick introduction to the American Do-si-do step. Shouts and clapping rocked the shelter! Music is international, crossing barriers, joining all people, and so it was this afternoon. The Kitchen Band would come several more times to the delight of staff, volunteers and the residents of the shelter.

There were other dances held once a month under strict supervision of Captain Holcomb and the staff. Local college students sponsored them and served snacks and soft drinks. Some families, in their cubicles, covered their ears wondering why this Western culture music needed to be played so loud. It was an outlet for the young people of Central America and they greatly enjoyed each and every dance.

Wednesday, April 15

During the day I would be greeted in the living quarters with smiles, hugs and small arms clinging to me. There were squeals of delight as I peeked around corners in the game of hide and seek. I enjoyed this game as much as the little ones, for their sparkling black eyes and brilliant smiles warmed my heart. I was learning step by step. I gave them a smile, a cheerful greeting and showed respect, and in return I gained their trust.

However, mothers found themselves confined day in and day out by their children, so it was arranged that children of the ages, for first grade up to sixth would spend mornings at Saint Peter's school in Plattsburgh and Saint Alexander's in Morrisonville. They would be brought by the shelter van in the morning, share lunch with the local children, then be picked up by the shelter van. It proved to be quite an experience for the area students who took them under their wing. Perhaps in a small way they understood a little more about the world they lived in. The younger children, ages two to four years, were transported to the Methodist Day Care Program in Plattsburgh several times a week. Central Americans, are very protective of their children. Often a mother would accompany them for the few hours they spent in the morning at the day care center. This was a small reprieve for the mothers who could then write a letter, do wash, or just have quiet moments for themselves which made for a happier family.

To occupy the children's time in the afternoon a local art teacher, Meredith O'Connor, came after lunch several times a week with her art supplies to do craft projects. The children looked forward to the arrival of this special lady who helped them create beautiful art work in their barren world.

Meredith soon expanded their talent under her artistic guidance. The drab sheetrock walls of cubicles that surrounded the dining area were transformed. Older children and talented, artistic men took part in creating and bringing the beauty of life into the living quarters. Murals showing deep feelings and hope were brought to life for all to enjoy. One mural depicted Christ in a boat with his disciples, another the world with children of different races and cultures with joined hands, and outlining the top a phrase over and above them: "We are the World . . . We are the Children."

Thursday, April 16

What a wonderful, happy surprise for George when Walid arrived! They had known one another as students at the American University in Lebanon, five years ago. There were tears of happiness as George told what had taken place in his life and Walid told George how he had gone to Germany to find work. However, he was unable to receive permanent working papers and had to leave. They asked me if it was possible to call their mothers in Lebanon from one of the phones in the main office. I said I would check, and to our surprise the Salvation Army staff member said, "Yes, just get time and charges after the calls." As a mother I understood the words of love reaching across oceans into the heart of a mother who did not know where her son was or where he was going. It surely was a small world! To meet after five long years at a shelter in the town of Plattsburgh.

Friday, April 17

A large dispensing machine was provided by Bay View Dairy of Cumberland Head for the milk purchased from them. Now the children and adults could have cereal rather than doughnuts for breakfast. But more important, children could have all the milk they wanted in addition to the one small bottle of juice that was handed out individually to them. How I wished at times I could give juice to all. Sometimes I did when they were sick, without staffs' knowledge. Owned by the Brandell family, the dairy also made its own ice cream and on several occasions donated enough ice cream to treat the 183 to 185 people that now resided at the shelter. What a treat it was, from the very youngest to the oldest resident!

Another family-owned business gave from their heart. Fruit was desirable and would be eaten before any baked goods. Cindy Pytlak of Pytlak Orchards brought bushels of fresh apples to the shelter several times. They disappeared almost before she left the parking lot.

Three balanced meals were now being served at the shelter. At times the Sri Lankans asked to cook their traditional dishes. The Central Americans were not too happy, for they would tell us, "They are dirty, they don't shower. They just wash their hair and feet in the sink." As a result, international signs, with pictures of washing hair and feet with a slash mark drawn through them, were made and posted over sinks in all bathrooms.

In any case, volunteers who accompanied the Sri Lankans

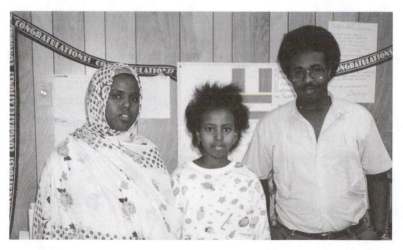

Ethiopian woman and her daughter with a man from Saudia Arabia. Emergency Salvation Army Shelter, Town of Plattsubrgh, 1987.

to the kitchen said, "They are very clean in handling and preparing the meals." Still, not many refugees would eat on the days they cooked, but instead ate a lot of bread and fruit. However, the staff and volunteers, including me, greatly enjoyed the different "curry" tasting meal. We learned to have a large cold drink on hand. It was hot!

For the true practicing Moslem, the most Holy Season Ramadan begins in March. It is the period of time (depending what night the crescent moon was seen and proclaimed in the Middle East in the ninth month of the Mohammedan year) when the Archangel Gabriel gave a message to Mohammed and Mohammed wrote the Koran. It is a time of strict fast and abstinence from food, drink and water from sunrise to sunset for the 30 days. At the shelter their dinner plate was kept in the refrigerator for them until they could eat. Not all Moslems were this strict in their faith, but many, in the privacy of their cubicles, knelt and prayed five times a day, facing the East. I walked in unexpectedly one day and with an "excuse me," retreated hastily, feeling I had intruded in a most personal way.

Some Moslems would not take animal or dairy products, some were vegetarians, yet others ate beef and chicken, but very few ever ate pork.

They respected our Christian faith and were very interested in learning about it. I was asked many questions and asked questions in return. I was learning! And we were understanding one another through communication and respect.

Friday, April 24

Noemi, George and Walid had left for Montréal. Oscar and eight other refugees were the last group I transported with the van in late April to the border. We would miss Oscar deeply for he had given his time and effort in so many ways.

When needed, he translated at doctor appointments or for the interviewing of new arrivals, and did extra menial work when asked, such as mopping the men's bathroom floor, in addition to doing a superb supervisory job. He was always ready to help in any way. He was one of the very few refugees I ever took to my home and introduced to my friends.

I remember the day I brought him home and the pleasure he took in the view of the lake while enjoying simple refreshment, a view that we take for granted. He was inquisitive and interested in what John's work entailed as planner at NYSEG (layout for requested commercial/residential power, transmission lines, drawing of plans and cost of project).

Oscar told how transmission lines were the favorite target of the guerrillas especially the one leading to the capital San Salvador. The city would be without power for many hours and sometimes days. Again we take for granted the quick response to and repair of any outages by linecrews.

Oscar was very concerned that the shelter would close before his wife and three daughters would arrive, which was to be sometime in May. There were statements in the *Press-Republican* by Commissioner Pandozy that the A.R.C. hoped to have its building back by May. Everyone thought of the shelter as only temporary emergency housing and that the flow of refugees would slow or stop.

Oscar said he would keep in touch with me regarding his family. He did so with letters and then his phone call to tell me he expected his family between May 12 and 22. I told him, "Rosemary and I will be here to welcome them."

Tuesday, April 28

The privately owned businesses in Plattsburgh were always willing to give of their services or products, sometimes even before being approached. This was clearly the case at Easter time.

Joann's Nuthouse, a candy kiosk located in Pyramid Mall, donated assorted Easter candy baskets and chocolate bunnies to the children at the shelter. Needless to say, there were happy, contented children for days after. Many did not know or understand the Christian tradition, but they sure knew the wonderful taste of chocolate!

When Sue Steuart's son Andy, was volunteering at the shelter and heard about a refugee's upcoming birthday, a decorated ice cream cake was made at Dairy Queen and given to the person on the special day. There was much given and love shared, sometimes in large ways, more often in smaller ways. It was the hospitality of the North Country at its best!

Thursday, April 30

Although there never was a serious problem at the shelter, it wasn't all honey and roses. There were several cases of shop-lifting but they were resolved amicably. There were several case of social problems. For instance, a young Hispanic man who looked a little too long at a young girl from another culture brought a complaint by her father to me. A young Hispanic man making advances towards a young girl of his culture would send the mother looking for that young man to give him a tongue-lashing that you could hear throughout the shelter. I would turn to Lt. Judy to handle these problems. It's called passing the buck.

There was the case of the "little white car." Girls were appearing in a "little white car" while the men played soccer in the large, back parking lot. Kathy and Barb went out to tell them, "This is private property, please leave." They did, but came back that night, so Lloyd, in no uncertain terms, told them to leave or the next time the troopers would greet them. End of the "little white car." At night, every half hour or so, the outside of the building was patrolled to be sure no one was loitering.

Alcohol was finding its way into the shelter on occasion and it got to be a "cat and mouse" game between staff and the young men.

Then came the day when I came face to face with the true meaning of "macho" behavior. We never knew, among those who came through, who were rebel force members or political foes. We were just there to help. Jose always dressed in fatigue clothing down to army boots. He had problems! What, I did not know nor did I care to know. One day he went flying out the door with Kathy and Barb right behind him. As good a runner as Kathy was, Jose disappeared around the back of the shelter, over the fence and into the woods. Kathy said to me, "If he comes back and wants his personal things, he is to come to me first." So it was noted in the night/day log book for the night shift. Two days later around noon, I saw Jose squatting down near the front door. I went out and told him Kathy wanted to see him. He didn't want to go in, she would have to come out. In I went to give Kathy the message. She said, "No, he is to come in." There is no rule that a refugee must stay at the shelter. He can leave anytime he wants. Out I went to give Jose Kathy's message. He said he didn't want to go in because Nancy Tyrell, from Salvation Army, was manning the front desk. I was puzzled by that. "Why?," I asked.

"She doesn't like me. She will say something to me," he said from his sitting position. In I went to ask Nancy not to say anything to him so he would come in to see Kathy. Nancy was as puzzled as I by his request but agreed. Out I went and told Jose, "Nancy isn't going to say anything, just follow behind me." He still hesitated. Then I made my blooper. In a rather harsh voice I said, "Act like a man that has a backbone and go in."

I hardly had "go in" out of my mouth when he shot up, coming face to face with me, eyes blazing and said, "I am a man!" I stood still, did not step back, held my ground and came back in a gentler voice, "Show me by coming with me." He did, with one hand on my shoulder. He followed close behind me as we walked passed Nancy to where Kathy was waiting. Jose stayed in the shelter until his entry date into Canada. It was the first time I was a little frightened. I learned a very important lesson that day: don't challenge an Hispanic's manhood.

At lunchtime, as in the other shelters, two lines were formed, one for men, and one for women and children. Women and children were served first. On this particular day I was on my way to the main office through the dining area, when I heard heated words in Spanish among the men in line. I stopped and asked what was wrong. Several men told me that five young Hispanic men always cut to the front of the line at lunch time. I asked the chief cook if this was true and he said, "Yes." I proceeded to the front of the men's line where the five were and asked, "Is this true?" Of course I got a "no" with grumbling from the other men. I stood in front of them and said, "I am sorry but no one will be served until all of you go to the end of the line. I am willing to stay here however long you wish it to be." They stood there for what seemed like five minutes, then to my relief they went to the back of what was now a long line of men. The appreciation resounded with "muchas gracias" and "thank you" as I continued on to the main office.

Thursday, May 14

This evening a special party was given by the Hispanics at the shelter to thank the volunteers and to honor mothers on Mother's Day. They had decorated the main office with bouquets of silk flowers and a large handwritten card that was inscribed:

To all volunteers
with love

from the Hispanic
people of the shelter.

Posted in the main office, the following poem, roughly translated:

Mother, Oh my mother! Now in this glorious
day let the peace and the love reign in your heart.
This is one of your instincts of greatness and
the much love of your son. I beg to Lord of the
Heaven to bless and to conserve always.
Live mother of my life.

With love to the mothers.

E.J.A.
El Salvador

In the dining area was a huge sign they had used as a large backdrop. They had written in Spanish:

Feliz Dia—HAPPY DAY
Madres De—MOTHERS FROM
Todo El Mundo—ALL THE WORLD

We were serenaded in song and enjoyed music and humorous skits that brought a mixture of tears and laughter. I need not add anything, for they said it all from their hearts.

Friday, May 15

There was another change in officers with the arrival of Captain Kathy Douglas from Syracuse in late April. She and I developed a warm relationship, for I found myself in the "living quarters" each day working with her as her assistant. It was very seldom I would drive, unless no one else was available.

She was a very compassionate young lady not only towards the refugees, but also the volunteers under her. Captain Kathy did not hesitate to ask for advice if she did not know or understand how things were run. She was always willing to listen to any suggestions that we might have. In fact she would ask one of us before going to Captain Holcomb. She was also frustrated by having to beg for the basic necessities for the shelter. She was always told, "you have it there" when we didn't, or "the volunteers must be taking it."

I was so upset when I heard this, I left the shelter, got in my car and went to see Captain Holcomb. He had always said, "My door is always open. Come and see me if there is a problem." By the time I arrived at the Salvation Army building, about six miles away, I still felt upset. Ginger told me he was there and to go right in.

I walked in and said, "Captain, I almost felt I had to walk around this building three times before I came in to see you."

"Please sit, Fran, and tell me what is wrong."

I told him how the volunteers had to beg for necessities, of hearing the accusations of volunteers stealing, of his not listening to problems and addressing them, to the frustration of everyone. After all, he had made it perfectly clear he was the one in charge. "Where have you been?" I thought to myself. No one saw him unless it was with political leaders or news reporters. Of course I didn't tell him that, but everyone knew it to be true.

I told him how some refugees had come to me, not staff, with problems that concerned them, how I had relayed these problems to the proper staff members and nothing had been done. He asked what I thought would help. I responded by offering to take inventory each and every day and report directly to Ginger. It would confirm what was there and what was needed. I suggested that he call a meeting with the refugees and address another problem. Families were sleeping with pieces of two-by-fours across their doors. They were frightened at night by the noise and roaming of young men throughout the halls. He agreed.

When I returned to the shelter everyone thought I had quit. Kathy was concerned over what had happened. I said, "He could have told me to leave, but he didn't." We only hoped things would become better.

Barb and I spent Sunday afternoon taking inventory of items ranging from toothpaste to brooms.

When a staff opening came about, Captain Holcomb offered it to me, but I declined without regret. I was more than happy where I was, with the people. Joan Studebaker was hired for the night shift.

Lloyd was now part-time on the day shift and he could see things had changed. There was difficulty filling the position of supervisor to make up and oversee the crews. There seemed to be a different caliber of young men coming through, who did not want the responsibility. If one did take the position he was not respected by the others. The entries from the night/day log showed an increase in rowdiness during the night. The one big change was the "policing" by the refugee team that had not been replaced when the last team left in early May for Canada.

Monday, May 18

Today while I was at work, the phone rang at my home. With luck, John had taken a vacation day and was at home. It was Cora, Oscar's wife, calling from the border. She and her three daughters, Maria, Erika, and Sandra, had been there since 7:30 a.m. and would be taking the 1:00 p.m. bus back to Plattsburgh. John called the shelter to leave the message for me.

Rosemary and I each took our own car and left for the border at noon, arriving before the bus had left. I had no idea what Oscar's wife looked like, but saw an attractive lady with two pretty, black-haired girls (Erika and Sandra) standing near the bus. I walked over and asked if she was Cora. "Yes, are you Fran?" Maria, the third daughter, was inside the building. She emerged, a pretty, blond eighteen-year old with greenish eyes who spoke great English. Erika understood but was very shy. What a lovely family!

They hastily loaded their luggage in our cars with Maria riding with Rosemary. We returned to the shelter, chatting like dear friends.

Rosemary and I had cleaned an empty cubicle earlier and decorated it with a welcome sign in the family quarters. Cora and the girls were not only surprised by our appearance at the border, but also by our thoughtfulness in making them feel welcome. Rosemary and I had been impatiently waiting for weeks to meet Oscar's family, so for us it was like greeting long lost relatives. Indeed, as the days went by they became like family members.

Wednesday, May 20

I arrived at my usual time, 6:30 a.m., and routinely read the night/day log before entering the "living quarters." I found a lengthy entry by Tom Middleton of the night staff about a problem that had occurred at 2:00 a.m.

A woman from Peru had an epilepsy attack and her screaming had awakened everyone in the shelter. Tom, a trained Emergency Medical Technician, found her with her head pinned in a down position, between the cot and wall. He gave immediate medical treatment, saving her life. He then called for an ambulance to transport her to the hospital, where she was admitted.

I found Cora alone in the dining area waiting for me. She was frightened and upset. She told me, "The Devil came in the middle of the night." Cora's cubicle was directly across from where the crisis had taken place.

Cora is an educated lady, a teacher. Yet, for the people

66

that night, an evil entity had come. They never understood that it was a medical problem that could be treated. Even after the woman was released and returned to the shelter with medication, everyone avoided her. They thought she was possessed by something evil.

Thursday, May 21

The plan to close the shelter on May 27th had been postponed with the increase of refugees arriving. There are now 150 housed at the shelter. Since the building must be turned over to the ARC no later then June 12th, the Interfaith Council met with their group of volunteers to develop a host home network to privately care for the refugees. It would be set up and headed by the volunteer coordinator, Margot.

Monday, May 25

Memorial weekend was drawing near and the spring days were fresh and warm. Nancy Tyrell, staff member of Salva-

Memorial Day picnic at volunteer Sue Steuart's home. 1987.

tion Army, felt "spring fever." While on duty one day she suggested having a picnic for the refugees on the 25th. The volunteers on duty thought it was a great idea, but where could we hold it with 150 refugees and the many volunteers? It would be the first big summer holiday of the year for Americans and they would fill the state parks. Wheels began to turn when Sue Steuart offered her home with acres of open land. Plenty of room! Word went out and volunteers came forward providing lawn games, baseball equipment, badminton sets, volley and soccer balls. They prepared all kinds of salads, with the Salvation Army providing the many pounds of hamburger, hot dogs, buns, rolls, condiments and potato chips from their supplies and transporting all this in their truck. An eight-foot barbecue grill had to be made in order to cook the hamburgers and hot dogs to serve this many people.

Sue contacted Rulf's Orchards in Peru and they donated apples. She called the Pepsi-Cola Company in Keeseville and they provided, at cost the soft drinks, setting up and taking down their soft drink dispenser. Again we saw the generosity coming from North Country hearts. Buses from the Bible Baptist Church and the two shelter vans, transported everyone from the closed shelter. Nancy, who had suggested this wonderful idea, stayed to secure the empty building. Nancy showed, once again, her concern and love "for those so far from their homeland."

Teams made up from different cultures played against one another in volleyball and soccer games, with the young Sri Lankan girls playing the less strenuous badminton. Children chased each other and their laughter and squeals filled the air. They ran through fields just for the sheer joy of it. In a tractor-drawn wagon hayrides were happily given by Sue's son Andy. Others just sat in circles talking, feeling the warmth of the spring day. Everyone feasted from a laden table as often as they wished.

All refugees had full use of Sue's home. She did not put one valuable item away. Loose change lay in full view on a table and not one thing was taken. These people of all cultures showed their great respect to this special American hostess and her husband Bernie.

This day was shared in friendship and peace, with memorable hours passing all too quickly. Soon they would return to the shelter where Captain Holcomb would hold an unannounced meeting to address unacceptable behavior. Upon everyone's return to the shelter an announcement was made over the loud speaker. There would be a meeting at 7:00 p.m. and everyone was to attend. Sue's and my efforts to hold such a meeting had finally been realized.

There was a lot of chatter among the refugees who were wondering what this meeting was all about. They knew the shelter was to close. They wondered if they would be informed tonight.

Captain Holcomb appeared in full dress uniform promptly at 7:00 p.m. Many squirmed in their seats as he walked into the dining area, for when he appeared they knew it was serious.

A volunteer was asked to come forward as an interpreter. No one moved! It now had reached a point in the shelter that if anyone was to help the "gringos" in a supervisory position or any other way, a clique of young men would verbally abuse or give them a very hard time. One young man named Mourice stepped forward. He was small of build, very self-assured, almost cocky. Mourice had seen and heard the rowdy nights. He had arrived last week just a few days before his wife and young son left for Montréal. I had seen Mourice stand eye-to-eye with larger young men when he thought they were doing something wrong. Captain Kathy had to come in to mediate these problem.

The 30– to 40–minute meeting began with Captain Holcomb saying, "I speak to the few young men who are disturbing the many in this building. There are rules here and everyone is expected to obey them. If you can't or don't want to, there is the door. Leave. You are not held here against your will, you are free to walk out right now and be on your own. We are here to help, but I will not allow the few to think the rules do not apply to them."

He went on to address the damages done. The holes between the men's and women's showers, the holes between the empty and women-occupied cubicles. "Sleeping all day and rowdiness at night are finished," he said. "Everyone will be up by nine o'clock unless sick. You will be expected to do your share of work if asked. We are not here to babysit you nor to wait on you." He added, "All packages will be inspected more closely and any item that looks suspicious will also be inspected closely before being allowed into the living quarters."

Then he asked if everyone was present. Melissa, an evening staff member, said, "No, Carlos is in his cubicle." As this space faced the dining area, we knew Carlos had heard everything. He was one of the young men taking part in the night problems. Captain Holcomb went to Carlos's cubicle. Carlos emerged shortly after, but the Captain didn't. After what seemed like ten minutes, Captain reappeared holding a quart bottle of liquor. He walked very slowly through the dining area, with all eyes on him. Entering the men's bathroom, which directly faced the dining area, he opened the bottle and ever so slowly poured the contents down the sink. He came out holding the empty bottle high and dropped it into a trash can. A loud bang was heard throughout the hushed dining area. He went on to say, "If anyone has a drinking problem or a problem with these perverse actions, come and see me. I will be more than happy to counsel you."

He then turned to where staff and the few volunteers were sitting and asked "Anything else?" I replied, "Yes. Please tell the men to not bother the young girls. Leave them alone." A Sri Lankan father had come to me at the picnic to point out that Carlos was bothering one of his daughters.

"You heard her, I heard her and if I hear any more on this, you will be thrown out of the building," said the Captain. End of meeting.

The "security team" was reactivated. Men were chosen, times were set up and the team was headed by Mourice. Nights were once again peaceful.

Thursday, May 28

I first noticed her engrossed in reading, sitting alone at an empty table in the dining area. There was an aura of mystery, dignity and class that held me from intruding into her world. I had seldom seen her, but at the festive picnic I saw her taking pictures, stopping to speak with Sue, and realized she spoke English. Still I did not approach her.

A few days later she asked for a clean sponge to clean her cubicle, which I gave her. Later that afternoon I was to take Rosemary to a local garage to pick up a repaired van and then have a prescription filled. The woman again approached me and asked if I was going anywhere near a place that she might buy an inexpensive frame for a drawing she had done. I told her about a department store in the same plaza as the pharmacy.

On the way, Rosemary and I found out her name was Parvin and she was from Iran. She liked to draw and wanted to buy a frame for one drawing to give as a gift. On returning to the shelter, Parvin asked if I would like to see what she had done in the two and a half weeks she had been here. Two and a half weeks? It was only last week that I first saw her. I followed Parvin into a clean, neatly organized cubicle where she took out several exquisite, colorful, penciled drawings, one of a couple strolling among flowers, another of a woman attending a flower garden, but a particular one caught my eye. It was a side view of a nude lady, done in black pencil, in a sitting position with her head on her arms on drawn up knees. It radiated total desolation and despair. I asked Parvin when she had done this and she said, "Last week."

Parvin was sitting on the floor and she started crying, almost uncontrollably. I was taken aback in surprise! I had never had this happen to me before. I didn't know what to do! Instinctively I took her hand in mine and listened as she tried, between sobs, to tell me of leaving a very sick mother with heart problems. She had stayed in California with relatives but left before her visa ran out to apply for entry into Canada. She had not spoken to her mother in three weeks because of security reasons. She was an only child and her mother was a widow. She didn't mind the shelter or the noise, only that in her mind she could hear her mother calling her name in the darkened night. After her outpouring, which I am sure I did not completely understand, Parvin calmed down somewhat. In soft tones, I told her she could send for her mother once she was settled in Canada. It seemed so inadequate to one in such turmoil. Parvin was to leave next week, June 7th, and I had just met her. Still, it proved to be a turning point in my life.

Wednesday, June 3

Each spring I work at Beekmantown School Registration for voting on the budget. However, this year it was late and held in early June. I called the Superintendent's office to ask his secretary Carol Sanger if Maria and Erika could come with me to see an American school and perhaps attend the Spanish class. Carol thought it was a great idea. When I told Maria and Erika they were very excited, but I said they would have to get permission from their mother. Cora said, "OK, because

72

I trust you, Fran."

Sitting with Mary Fogarty, a fellow worker, and me, they scrutinized every Beekmantown student that came by and how they were dressed. The thorough "once-over" seems to be the norm of young people the world over. Maria said, "The school is larger than our Albert Einstein University." She had been a first year student there. Erika, with Sandra, had attended a private German school.

A young girl by the name of O'Malley came by and offered to take them on a tour of the school. When they returned, Maria and Erika were very excited about what they had seen. Our gym was even larger than the stadium at Maria's former university.

They went off to have lunch with Carmen Culver, the Spanish teacher, and then to attend her class. We learned upon their return that lunch was a banquet compared to the shelter's. Maria added, "I didn't understand very much in the Spanish class. The Spanish taught here is different from ours." She and Erika greatly enjoyed visiting with the students and answering questions about El Salvador.

It had been arranged that Rosemary would come to pick them up. I was not surprised to see Cora and Sandra with her. Rosemary had taken them along to see some of our North Country beauty.

John and I brought Cora and the girls to our home, where on one occasion they made tacos for dinner. Later the girls took a canoe ride for the first time in their lives. John and Maria would sit by the hour and discuss the engineering field, an area of study that Maria was interested in, and the engineering universities here.

We took Erika and Sandra into our hearts, but it was Maria's outgoing personality and liveliness with her unending questions that made the hours spent together seem like minutes.

So began a dear friendship with this family that flourishes more with each passing day.

Thursday, June 4

The week before the shelter was to close, Captain Kathy's fiance James was to arrive around noon. Everyone was anxious to meet this young man about whom we had heard so much. With Nancy's instigation, a surprise bridal shower had been planned to be held that evening at Sue's home. James knew about it.

I was to talk Captain Kathy into taking a ride to show her and James some of the sights of the area, arriving at Sue's at 7:30 p.m. I approached Captain Kathy about the idea and since James was in on this he said, "I would like that very much." I picked them up at 6:45 and drove along Lake Shore Road south to Clinton Community College. We marveled at the scenic view laid out before us. We continued on south past a local marina that brought "ooh's and aahs." Soon we were approaching Sue's home and I suggested stopping. As we pulled into the driveway only Sue's car was visible. All others had been parked out of view.

As Sue let us in, "Surprise!" echoed through the kitchen. Indeed, Captain Kathy was surprised when she saw the decorations and the 15 or so volunteers who were there. She was even more shocked when she found out that James was in on it.

Dishes of crackers, cheese and finger foods laded the lace-covered table, adorned with a beautiful silver bowl filled with punch. A delicious cake made by Anna from Peru, South America, was the topping to a wonderful evening. Anna, with her two children and husband, sister-in-law Rosa and her two children, were being hosted by Sue and her husband Bernie. Sue and Bernie's was the first home to host a family.

Time passed quickly, with beautiful gifts being opened by a still-surprised, grateful, deserving young lady. The evening ended with my stopping on the way home at Valcour Lodge, a lovely restaurant overlooking Lake Champlain, to share a non-alcoholic nightcap with a very happy couple.

Saturday, June 6

Cora and her girls would be leaving for their entry date on Monday, June 8th. John and I had thoroughly enjoyed their company often at our home. Now we wanted them to taste and experience an old-fashioned American barbecue before they left. So with our neighbors, the Gilligans, we planned to bring them to our home where we would enjoy a farewell cook-out together.

After our first meeting I had seen Parvin several times and spoken with her. I felt how lonely and sad she was and on speaking with Cora I found this to be true. Cora had met Parvin shortly after she had arrived. Drawn to her because she too saw what turmoil Parvin was feeling, they had become friends. I decided to invite Parvin to the barbecue also and she agreed to come. She would be leaving for Montréal tomorrow, June 7th.

Barb and I made potato and macaroni salads, baked beans, jello, hot rolls and fresh corn on the cob. Jim, Barb's husband, brought his grill over and, with John, cooked the chicken. In the ice chest there were all kinds of soft drinks. I knew Parvin was Moslem, and I mentioned to her that the dish of beans was flavored with strips of bacon. However, she partook and greatly enjoyed them with all the other dishes, saying how good everything was. After the shelter meals I guess it would be!

The day was warm and sunny with clear blue skies. The lake was rippled by a light southern breeze. A perfect day. Cora and girls, the Gilligan family and John played a no-rules, hot game of volleyball. Maria and her sisters were good. It was soon apparent volleyball was not Parvin's cup of tea. I saw her wander off with her camera taking pictures of our flowers. Then she walked toward the lake where I found her sitting near the shore.

I sat with her and we talked. I learned she had been a teacher of philosophy as well as other related subjects for a number of years. She taught not only at a private school but at government-run school, which we would consider prep or junior college. She held Masters degrees, not only in philosophy but also psychology. With tears in her eyes she changed the subject abruptly to how beautiful it was here. I did not push to find out anything more about her. We spoke about everything and nothing, sitting alone undisturbed for over an hour with only the gentle lapping of water against the rocky shore. Then it was time to take everyone back to the shelter for the doors are locked at 10:00 p.m. One needed a pass in order to stay out later. Besides, Parvin had to finish packing for her departure tomorrow.

Would I ever see her again? I did not know. However, Parvin had opened my world to feelings I never was aware of before. She expanded my outlook on life with the beginning of a unique friendship that begins and ends in our hearts.

Monday, June 8

It was 6:00 a.m., a dark rainy Monday morning when I arrived early to take a surprised Cora, Maria, Erika and Sandra to the border. After all, I had gone to pick them up when they first arrived. They were to take the Greyhound bus but quickly agreed that I take them. I would be back, I assured the night staff, to start my shift at 7:30 a.m. Paul Cote would cover for me.

Since it was such a miserable morning I did what none of us were supposed to do. I parked my car in front of the entrance door on what was now a very soggy lawn. The spare tire had to be taken out in order to put the luggage in since there was only one car making the trip. While loading, who walked in totally unexpected but Captain Holcomb. "Fran, whose car?"

"Mine, Captain; I will be gone in a matter of minutes." He wasn't too happy and told me as much. However, I was gone with Cora and the girls in less than two minutes. The car had never been packed so quickly.

Cora was worried about me, not only because of Captain Holcomb's attitude, but the possibility of my not being back in time for my shift. I told her, "No problem," and there wasn't, but there were ruts left in the lawn.

It was so hard to say good-bye. Cora had my telephone number and Parvin had Cora's. I hoped to keep in touch in a round-about way, for I didn't know where Parvin was staying in Montréal.

On my return I found posted on the wall of their cubicle a colorful hand-drawn card saying, "Thanks to Fran, Captain Kathy, Kathy Mc., Rosemary, Kathy C., Aunt Nancy." It was signed by Cora and the girls. I removed it as my personal keepsake.

For the last time I rounded up a crew to clean the outside area around the building. Others were busy cleaning the inside, folding cots and blankets and storing them. Tonight would be the last night spent in the shelter that had been home to so many. The Town of Plattsburgh and private businesses came to pick up their loaned equipment: ping pong table, weights, satellite dishes and TVs.

The nurse's supplies and clinic equipment had already been moved to space made available back at the Salvation Army building. The leftover items, from toothpaste to baby food, paper products and cleaning supplies, were also returned to the Salvation Army building.

A room for drivers to report, equipped with a telephone, would also be at the Salvation Army building. A log book would be used for each driver to check in/out with any important notes posted for the next driver. We would work out of the Army building with Margot calling us from her office at Catholic Charities. Margot would direct us to where we would be needed—picking up of new arrivals, transporting to the Crisis Center, doctor appointments, etc. My days spent as a volunteer would drop from five or six days to three. Now I was only driving.

Wednesday, June 10

So it came to pass, the closing of the shelter. Kathy Champagne coordinated and directed the move for the final 38 refugees living there. Shortly after 1:00 p.m., June 10th, Barb and I made several trips to and from the shelter to the Dawn Motel on Lake Shore Road South transporting the last

Kathy Champagne (social services), Captain Kathy Douglas (officer in charge of shelter), and volunteer Barbara Gilliagan. Emergency Salvation Army Shelter, Town of Plattsburgh. 1987.

residents. They had come full circle, for it was in motels in late 1986 that the refugees had first been housed.

The Salvation Army truck, driven by Tom Middleton, moved baby cribs and luggage to the motel with loading and unloading done by refugee men. Other men swept cubicles, halls and the dining area for the final time.

When I returned to the now empty building, Captain Kathy and I took one last walk around the living quarters, each deep in our own thoughts and memories. I could almost hear an echo of laughter, feel the liveliness, the despair, the hope of the hundreds this building once embraced. I saw shadows at the now empty tables of the many Plattsburgh residents who came to visit or just to play cards with the lonely. I heard the footsteps of the caring volunteers who numbered almost three hundred before the closing. Volunteers not only from Plattsburgh and the surrounding area but also from downstate New York, Vermont, and Canada. Now, there was only an eerie silence. The murals are to be preserved, local agencies say, but I do not know where.

Saying good-bye to this special lady, Captain Kathy, was difficult. We had become close associates. She really cared for the welfare of the refugees under her wing, but she was looking forward to returning to her home and her upcoming wedding. Gathering a few items, I said good-bye with eyes glistening, turned and walked out without looking back. The door closed on another phase of this program as a new one began. What would it hold for me?

Friday, June 12

Although the state had given an additional $40,000 to Social Services in the relief effort, refugee housing had to be found after the closing of the shelter. Some refugees rented small rooms in boarding homes or at the Dawn Motel. Those on Social Services were housed at the Dawn Motel and single young men were sent to Salvation Army shelters in the Utica or Syracuse areas. However, host homes were desperately needed for those that had no resources or place to go. It was a tremendous task taken on by Margot.

Sue and Bernie Steuart were one of the first families to open their home to host refugee families, an enlightening and rewarding experience that led to further hosting and close friendships. As other relatives arrived Sue got calls from Montréal seeking her help and she was always there for them. As Bernie once said with a smile, "I never knew who might be sleeping in my bed."

Their kindness was remembered in a special way with an invitation to "celebrate," in Montréal, the marriage of a young Somalian man who had been one of their guests. Sue commented on how interesting the ceremony had been and how welcomed she felt.

The following churches and religious homes (that I knew about) hosted or would eventually host; I am sure there were others: First Presbyterian, Brinkerhoff Street; United Methodist, Beekman Street; First Baptist—American, Court & Oak; Our Lady of Victory Convent, South Catherine Street; Saint John's Convent, 64 Court Street; Parsonage, Church of God, Tom Miller Road; Saint Joseph Rectory, Dannemora, and Saint Joseph Convent, Dannemora.

Pat Cote, Paul's wife, was a dedicated volunteer whose heart was full of sorrow for her fellow man. "These poor souls," as she referred to them. She always went out of her way to do little things for the refugees, such as making a cup of tea or coffee with extra sugar or giving them a ride to the mall.

She also knew Oscar, and when Cora arrived she became friends with the family. Often Pat took Maria in the van with her on rounds. On a return trip to the shelter one day, Pat stopped at her daughter Valerie's home to introduce Maria to Val and to Val's husband Mark. Val asked Maria to spend the afternoon with her. Cora, Sandra and Erika would also become friends with Val and Mark, but it was Maria who was extra special to the handicapped Val. When Cora and family joined Oscar in Montréal, Val and Mark would go every other weekend to visit. However, it was Maria who went with Val for walks, pushing Val in the wheelchair and spending special moments together.

And Meredith O'Connor, this wonderful, talented lady, continued her teaching at local motels after the shelter closed. Wherever the children were, she followed.

Tuesday, June 16

Rosemary was an occasional driver and while waiting for Margot's call one day in June she asked me, "When are we going to take a trip to Montréal to see Parvin?" Some volunteers were already going up to see their extended "families" in Montréal. We now knew where she was staying because Sue had brought Parvin's extra bags to her.

Parvin's first hearing had gone well. Like other new arrivals, she would be receiving a stipend from the Québec government within two weeks from that hearing. She would receive her permit to work after her second hearing, which for her would be in September. Until then she had to live on her small monthly check. For some with families or single young men and women it would prove to be very difficult.

Rosemary and I decided to go on a weekday when we both were free, taking Rosemary's youngest son Colin. We found downtown Montréal very confusing. We were thankful we had a city map with us. We finally found the Salvation Army building on Drummond Street. The problem was, it turned out to be the "main headquarters" of the Salvation Army in Montréal. We took courage and went to the information desk, where the officer gave us directions to the department that had the addresses of those housed in Montréal.

After showing my Salvation Army card and stating the reason why we wanted to locate Parvin, they turned to their computer. Within minutes they not only found where she lived, but called there, only to find she wasn't in. We were very disappointed. After many "thanks" for their help we decided to go to the Hotel Europa, which was down the street from "headquarters," where we knew others from Plattsburgh were staying.

We entered a large, pleasant looking lobby whereupon Jose stepped out of the elevator! He was the husband of Rosa, who had stayed at Sue's home. He had come to Montréal shortly before the closing of the shelter and before Rosa arrived in Plattsburgh. We asked if he had seen Parvin. "Yes, I know where she is now." She was with his wife at the Québec Immigration building. He had come from there to get additional paperwork that Rosa needed. So off we went, walking and chatting down ten blocks of Sainte-Catherine Street to Immigrations. It seemed a short distance on this beautiful day.

We went into a fairly large building, several stories high, that housed the particular Immigration Office we were going to, taking an elevator to the floor where it was located. We were only allowed at the front desk area, where we waited while Jose went into a larger room divided into cubicles.

Parvin appeared stunned when she saw us, bursting into tears as she embraced both of us. Between laughter and all of us talking at once, we must have appeared a very strange trio to the Immigration Officer, but I also saw a smile on his face. What a joyous reunion! Parvin told Rosemary, " I have used the umbrella you gave me the morning I left, many times. Thanks." I had not known that Rosemary had gone at six in the morning to see Parvin off! My new friend Rosemary was proving to be full of surprises. Turning to me Parvin said, "I have the gift you sent by Sue. I am keeping it packed until I have my own place." Now Rosemary gave me an amusing look and smile.

"Come, I want you to meet a friend." We followed her out the door and down the hall into a private office where we met Akbar, who worked for Immigrations. It was only a short meeting as he was quite busy, but I was taken by his warm smile and greeting. We returned to the office where Jose's wife was being interviewed and busily filling out Québec government forms.

In a short time Jose and Rosa, with many others we knew, came out from the inner cubicles. Akbar appeared just as we were all about to leave for the Hotel Europa for lunch. He gave his apartment keys to Parvin and invited Rosemary, Colin and me for dinner. Of course Parvin would cook. She glowed with happiness as we accepted.

On the return walk Colin did not feel well. He felt very warm. The men took turns carrying him on their shoulders back to the hotel. We were a joyous group as we walked down Sainte-Catherine Street.

The cafeteria where meals were served was in the basement of the hotel. It seemed the room was filled with every culture from the four corners of the world. Like all mothers, Rosemary was prepared with children's Tylenol, for now Colin had a fever. Lunch for Colin was a cold soda. Surprisingly for Rosemary and I, the meal was quite good. It consisted of tasty rice with pieces of chicken and fresh vegetables. Time passed quickly, for we had many questions and wanted to know how everything was going for them. They in turn asked about everyone in Plattsburgh. We told them Lloyd now had the job of processing new arrivals for the Crisis Center. Margot, Pat, Paul, Sue and the many others were fine. They wanted us to relay their "thanks" to everyone for all the help they received and also sent their love. They added they would never forget Plattsburgh, the "City of Love."

We took Parvin to where she was staying to pick up a few things and for her to let the staff know she would be out for the evening. I assumed the Salvation Army worked the same way in Canada as in the United States with check in/check out. Parvin was very excited about looking for her own apartment in the coming week.

Off we went to Akbar's apartment, talking about everything nonstop. We were like schoolgirls. When Akbar arrived at 5:30 dinner was almost ready. What delightful aromas permeated the air! He helped with the rest of the preparation and was a perfect host. Rosemary and I did not question how they happened to know each other. That came about during the wonderful Persian dinner (Sabzi Polo Mahe) of rice, deliciously prepared fish and fresh salad with a special dressing. Albar and Parvin had known each other as students at Teheran University where they had become good friends. By the time the dessert of fresh fruit was served, Rosemary and I felt completely at home.

Parvin wanted to be back by 10 o'clock, so with many "thanks," we regretfully said good-bye to this warm, kind man, hoping to see one another again in the near future.

On our return to the Salvation Army building, Faye, the night staff supervisor, cheerfully greeted us. She insisted she would serve us cookies and soft drinks in the living room. How could we refuse? It meant a little more time to spend with Parvin. Faye asked us how the program was now run in Plattsburgh, adding she would like to come down to observe the operation. I extended an invitation to her. She took my telephone number and said she would be in touch within the next couple of weeks.

Summer, 1987

Saturday, June 20

John and I saw Parvin again when we went to see Cora, Oscar and the girls for the first time. We all went in late evening, making a very surprised lady happy. As we were about to leave she asked me if I would bring a letter to Sue, "if not too much trouble."

"Yes, no problem." I replied.

Tuesday, June 23

I did not know how quickly or deeply my caring would be tested until I received a call from Cora. She told me she had just found out that Parvin's mother had passed away. Cora had the telephone number of the Iranian family with whom Parvin was now staying. Cora had called and spoken with Parvin, but Parvin was incoherent with grief. Would I please call Parvin?

I had not heard from Parvin since John and I saw her just three days ago. She had told me, "I will call you when I have found an apartment and have a telephone. It could be a while." I knew her mother was ill with a bad heart, but I was nonetheless surprised by this news. Parvin had given me a letter for Sue on Saturday. Sue told me later it was a request for Sue to somehow, through a doctor, obtain heart medicine that was no longer available in Iran. Of course Sue could not. She would need a prescription from a doctor. Oh the frustration and helplessness Parvin must have felt! Leaving a sick mother, being so far away, and there was nothing she could do. Parvin had not told me her reasons for leaving home. Only if volunteered by her (or any of the others I met) would I learn the reasons for coming, for I would never ask.

I picked up the phone and with a shaking hand I dialed, not knowing what to expect. A soft hello. I asked for Parvin and heard muffled voices in the background. Then a very weak voice said, "Hello."

"Parvin? This is Fran." Then, like a dam bursting forth from great pressure words between sobs flooded my ear, rambling words I could not follow, catching only, "My heart is torn out! I am on fire!" Her anguish crossed the miles, filling me. She was inconsolable with grief. I asked, "Where are you, Parvin? Give me your address. I will find you." I had to repeat, for she truly was incoherent. Then the soft voice of the lady who first answered came on, giving me her address with directions. I said, "I will come to see Parvin shortly." She replied, "You are most welcome to come." I did not sleep well that night.

Saturday, June 27

Today we went back to see Cora and family, bringing small kitchen gadgets as gifts to help them get started. Like other volunteers, who had eaten with, almost lived with those at the shelter, Cora and family had become more than friends. They were like our family. Cora had prepared a delicious traditional El Salvadoran, dinner of cole slaw and pupusas (a type of meat pancake) with tomato sauce. We had brought fresh fruit for dessert. Our conversation over lunch was about Parvin. Cora had found out that Parvin's mother had died the day Parvin had left Plattsburgh, June 7th.

Why had it taken so long for Parvin to find out? We had just seen her last Saturday. She was looking forward to finding her own apartment! Cora said, "I was told a friend of Parvin waited until a family who were his friends could take her in." That must have been Akbar, and this turned out to be true. He realized how devastated Parvin would be and he wanted her safe with someone he knew would take care of her.

Since I had Parvin's address and the directions, it was

decided we would all go over. Oscar, Cora, Erika, Sandy, Maria, John and I left by car over the Jacques Cartier Bridge to the South Shore area. It took us 45 minutes to locate the address in the suburbs, only to find no one home. I wrote a short note, leaving it between the doors for Parvin. I tried calling several times during the course of the evening, but there was no answer.

John and I left, planning another trip to come back to Cora's the following Friday with material for John to construct partitions, making several separate rooms. John would have Friday off, for the 4th of July fell on Saturday. We would be home to spend the holiday weekend with our son Chris and his family.

During the following week, Rosemary and I met several times at Nick's, a downtown Plattsburgh restaurant, for coffee. We discussed our great concern for Parvin, who had no family here. We knew only of her friend Akbar. Rosemary had also spoken with her and found her to be very, very upset. She, too, was worried. So began the closing of ranks to support a devastated friend.

Friday, July 3

Early Friday morning, with the necessary tools safely packed in the back of John's pickup truck, we went to a local lumber yard to purchase the materials needed for building the partitions. There was no problem when we declared the material at the border and we were soon back at Oscar's apartment. What seemed like a simple task turned out to be an all-afternoon project. However, they now had more privacy. While John and Oscar measured, sawed and hammered, I asked Cora how the French classes were going. Oscar had been taking classes since shortly after his arrival in late March. Classes were given free to new arrivals by the Québec government. You had to know the language if you planned to live and work in Québec. He was doing OK, but Cora and Maria were finding it a little hard. Since Erika and Sandra would be going to a public school in the fall, they would be taking French and math courses only for the first year. They were not looking forward to it.

In late afternoon I called Parvin. How pleased and happy she was to hear my voice. "Yes," she had found my note, but was disappointed she had missed me. Lila, with her husband Akbar and family, had taken her out for the day and into late evening. When it was learned we were in Montréal, she wanted John and I to stop on our way home. I explained we would be leaving shortly because John was tired and dirty. Parvin replied, "Just stop for a few minutes." God love her! She really wanted to see us, she needed us, but it was not to be. Parvin then told me she was planning a memorial service for her mother, not to be held in a mosque, but in the home where she was staying. She asked that I let Sue and Rosemary know when she called to let me know the date. Parvin said, "I would like all of you to come." "We would be honored to come," I replied.

Sunday, July 12

On a very hot, humid, mid-July afternoon, Rosemary, Cora and I journeyed from Cora's home to the South Shore. We were thankful for Rosemary's air-conditioned van.

This would be the first time that I had seen Parvin since the Saturday of last month when Oscar and family had gone with John and I to see her. I had called and spoken with her many times over the past few weeks, and I had heard her pain.

We did not know the protocol or customs of the ceremony or service that would take place this Sunday afternoon, only that it was important for us to give our respect to, and be with, our grieving friend. We knew of the Eastern custom of removing one's shoes on entering a home, and we were about to do so, when we were greeted with, "No. Please leave them on." I recognized this soft voice, I had spoken with this lady on the telephone. She introduced herself as Lila. As other Iranian friends arrived, I felt the warmth and respect given us, for they removed their shoes, leaving them in the foyer. I learned later, and practiced the same, that it was not only for cleanliness, but also because of the Persian carpets.

What a shock when we saw what was once a lovely, dignified, classy lady now standing before us. I never expected to see such a totally devastated person. Parvin looked completely defeated, a lost soul as she greeted me with tears welling in her eyes. She was dressed from head to toe in black; her complexion had a tinge of yellow. As I received a little longer than normal embrace, I heard a soft, deep, anguished groan. I could feel her quiver and how thin Parvin was. I truly did not believe she could hold up much longer.

Parvin proceeded to introduce us to the four or more that were present and to others as they arrived. Rosemary and I knew Akbar, who had had us for dinner only a short time ago. I had a chance to speak with him. "Yes," he knew about Parvin's mother when we were there for dinner. It had not been the right time to let her know something was wrong. He waited until he had made arrangements with his close friends, Lila and Akbar, to take her in. Did I see his eyes glisten as he told me? Yes, for he too knew and had been close to Parvin's mother, spending many hours in her home.

Sue Steuart arrived with her daughter Amy, son Andy and his wife Marisa. She also had with her Omar, Yusef and Albullah, Somalian friends, and Jose, whose wife Rosa had stayed with Sue. Faye was last to arrive. We were pleased to see her once again.

Our presence was not only a catalyst of comfort to Parvin, but also an honor.

The table was laden with 10 to 15 dishes which had been prepared by Parvin over a three day period. Because the July days had been so hot, she had prepared most of the food at Akbar's apartment in Montréal, not wanting to heat Lila's home with her cooking. She carried the food back on the Metrobus or in Akbar's car to Lila's home. Who else would do anything so considerate as this? I don't think I would.

Everyone was drawn to the framed 8" by 10" picture of a young woman alone with the Koran, the Moslem Holy Book, positioned in a prominent place on the table. Parvin had drawn in black pencil a picture of her mother from a wallet-sized photo. The woman was beautiful, a sister look-alike of Sophia Loren, the famous Italian actress.

I was aware of haunting music playing softly in the background. From a large silver tray Lila served glasses filled with clear liquid, each holding a spoon. I asked Shohreh, an attractive thirtyish Iranian lady who was seated next to me, was this part of the service? "No, it is just a refreshing drink made with water, vinegar, sugar and mint." OK, Fran. You may feel foolish, but you will never learn unless you ask. I could not drink all of the sweet tasting drink.

Then it was time to serve ourselves, for the meal was buffet-style. Rosemary, Sue and family, Cora and I took a tid-bit of everything from the multitude of dishes. We were willing to try a little of everything for we did not want to offend anyone, especially Parvin, who had worked so hard. In my case, I am always willing to try something once, perhaps not twice, but at least once. A special sweet dish called "Halva" had been made with sugar, flour and oil. Sue said to Parvin, "This is so interesting. How do you prepare it? It has its very own distinctive taste."

"I brown [scorch] flour in a pan first. Take sugar, add little water to it, mix into the flour. Add saffron, then oil and mix together. It is not cooked. It is served at memorial ceremonies, and on some religious holidays." Parvin said.

During the course of the meal Rosemary and I found some of the food very foreign to our American palate, including the Halva. Later, in months to come, Rosemary and I grew to enjoy and look forward to the many delicious Persian dinners which were graciously served in homes of Iranian friends.

Serving plates and a huge bowl containing fresh fruit were brought into the living room. It was a perfect complement crowning a gracious meal. Coffee and tea was also served. While partaking of the fruit Shohreh told me, "Parvin will be coming tomorrow to stay with my family as a baby-sitter to my two children." I was surprised but did not question her. I asked if I might call Parvin there. "Please do. You are most welcome to come and see her," she said as she jotted down her address and telephone number.

I glanced over at Parvin, who was sitting across the room from me. She started to cry with muffled sobs and no one moved! I was about to go to her when Sue rose and took a seat next to Parvin and took her hand in hers. Without missing a beat, Sue continued her conversation as if nothing had happened. But something had; a friend had responded to a friend's emotional helplessness.

People began to leave. Sue and family also departed. We planned to do the same, but Parvin asked us to stay just a little longer. The three of us stayed with Lila and Parvin and spoke quietly among ourselves until early evening, giving a little more support by our presences, and spending a little more time with our despairing friend.

"I will call you, Parvin," were my parting words.

Tuesday, July 14

My volunteer days became a routine of reporting by 9:00 a.m., to the Salvation Army building, where I would wait for

Margot's telephone call with instructions for the day. And, I might add, her instructions didn't always go accordingly.

On my first trip to the Dawn Motel in the morning, I would bring milk, cereal, sugar, coffee if needed, spoons and styrofoam cups and bowls. Maria "Cookie" Pelkey, manager of the Dawn Motel, would set up breakfast for self-service each morning in a little enclosed back porch.

Priorities for drivers were to bring any new arrivals to the Crisis Center, health screenings, doctor appointments, and pick up any prescriptions at the pharmacy. Drivers provided transportation to the Salvation Army for lunch and dinner where their cook prepared meals Monday through Saturday and made sandwiches for Sunday. They also transported refugees for English/French classes at Our Lady Of Victory Secretarial School (OLV) who were taught by Ann Allen and Sister Theresa Moan.

Throughout the day, errands were run whenever time allowed. Those who had laundry to do were brought from the motel to Our Lady of Victory School, where laundry facilities had been arranged by Margot. Thursday would prove to be one of my busier days. An 11 o'clock Spanish Mass was held in the morning by Father Roger Martin at Our Lady of Victory Convent Chapel. Mass was continued after the shelter closed, for it meant so much to these people and Father Martin.

Drivers would bring new arrivals to the Crisis Center, where Lloyd copied their papers, interviewed them regarding their resources, and helped them find affordable rentals or referred them to Margot for host homes or, if needed, to Kathy for Social Services assistance.

If anyone arrived without papers they had to go to Canadian Immigration at Blackpool, Québec to obtain a hearing entry date. It meant they would take a cab or walk to the bus station to take a bus to the border. No driver was allowed to transport unless the refugees were legally qualified to be in the program.

After being processed by Lloyd they would receive paralegal advice from one of the trained volunteers. Before the shelter closed the former District Attorney, Joseph Kelley, along with Melinda Lee from Vermont, were the paralegals. I would then transport them to Darlene at the Army building to be health-screened.

I would see Kathy on the days I volunteered at the motel. She now worked out of her car, going to the motel to interview those who might need Social Services or check those already in the programs. She really understood what field work meant now!

Monday, July 27

While having lunch, which was terrible at times, a young lady came out of Darlene's clinic whom I had not seen before. She appeared very frightened. Darlene told me she came from Lima, Peru and that her name was Maritza. The "coyotes" (illegal paid crossing agents) had taken everything she had except her wedding band and the few dollars she had hidden before they smuggled her across the Mexican-U.S. border. I saw she was wearing slacks that had holes in them. We learned they had been torn by running through the sagebrush in the middle of the night. Darlene had just finished treating the ugly scratches Maritza had on her arms and legs.

Margot came to interview Martiza for a host home and to buy necessary items for her at K-Mart. It was decided to send her to the convent in Dannemora. This turned out to be terrible for Maritza! Although she spoke broken English, she had no one to talk with as she was alone all day. Darlene had given Maritza her home telephone number and told her to call her anytime. Two days in the convent proved to be enough for her. It was a very distraught Maritza who called Darlene, asking if she might stay with her.

I received a call from Darlene, for she knew I was concerned about Maritza, asking if she kept Maritza for one week, would I do the same? "We are going away for a few days next week, but I will ask John," I told her.

Oscar's family and Parvin had come for a day, but no one had ever stayed with us. This would be a big step into the unknown for John and me. I had always gone home to my little world each night. I knew John's outlook had changed since he had met Oscar, his family, and Parvin as well. Were we willing to share our home and allow such an intrusion into our private lives? I felt I was, but was John? He could do no more than say no, right? But the answer was "yes."

I asked Margot if it was all right because we were not on the list as a host home. It was fine with her. As my supervisor she had come to know me well. Too well at times!

So it came to pass that this shy, lovely, young lady with black, flowing hair entered our lives. She would ride with me on days I worked and helped in any way. She became my own interpreter, sitting up front close to me. Maritza also made the best salads, but was not familiar with some of the modern appliances. She was very inquisitive, learned quickly and insisted on helping with monotonous chores. She beamed with pleasure on hearing my "muchas gracias." I was becoming spoiled!

As the days slipped by it seemed very natural to have her with us. It was nice having a young person in our home again. She greatly enjoyed the rural setting and our quiet talks in the evenings. Gradually I saw a change taking place. The sparkle in her eyes and the radiant smile that greeted us each morning brightening our day. She attended church with us each Sunday, looking forward to breakfast at Gus's Restaurant afterward.

When our son Chris and his family visited, Maritza was drawn to our grandsons. Mike, my daughter-in-law, had a built-in baby sitter at our home. But it was Ryan, our youngest grandson, who held a special place in her heart. He was the same age and appearance, nine months old, and with black hair and brown eyes, as Maritza's little girl, Laura, whom she had left behind.

She told me, with tears flowing, that it was too dangerous to take her little girl on a such a journey (she was on her way to join her husband Percy in Montréal. He had been a policeman in Lima caught between political forces). Besides, the "coyotes" would not allow her to take Laura on the crossing. Babies cry! Even if Maritza could have, it still would have been too much money. She was charged $1000. She paid $500 in Mexico and the balance immediately after the crossing into the U.S. They also took the one bag she was allowed.

Mike brought several outfits of clothing she no longer wore to Maritza a few days before she was to leave. Maritza was thrilled. Now she would have something nice to wear to meet her husband Percy, whom she had not seen in almost a year. Darlene came to take Maritza for her hearing entry date and then on to Montréal, where Percy was waiting impatiently. She looked lovely the day she left and so happy! There goes my heart again!

John and I went several times to see them. We dined on wonderful South American food, basking in their warm hospitality.

Monday, August 3

When Oscar's family and Parvin went to Montréal they took with them a part of my heart. It was hard to let friends go, even though I spoke often by phone with Cora and Parvin. They were very much on my mind. They had become precious friends about whom I worried.

Now I found myself backing away, no longer becoming too close to the problems of those coming through. Why? Because I knew I was becoming burned out.

Even though John and I would be going on vacation shortly, I still turned to Rosemary, who understood what I was going through. Meeting at Nick's, and after many cups of coffee, I came to realize that there is just so much one can give. From this sharing grew a warm, close friendship with Rosemary that flourished more with each passing day. Thank you my friend!

John's vacation came at a perfect time. In the second week of August we returned to where we had first camped with our sons 24 years before, near a beautiful lake in the depths of a forest in Maine. The summer days were cool, but our daily canoe outings, along waterways and shorelines, were filled with the serenity of nature. My nights were serenaded by the distant, lonely, calls of the loon as I reflected in solitude beside a dying campfire. And as the days gave way to time I felt the renewal of my being.

Friday, September 18

It was a warm, sunny day in late summer when I headed north to see Parvin for the first time since the memorial service. I was looking forward to seeing her, but as the miles sped by, my thoughts were on our phone calls over the past weeks. I would find her on occasion composed and at other times I knew she had been crying, hearing the deep sorrow in her voice. With each call there was an increase of closeness, of understanding that became very special across the miles. Today would be a time for just the two of us alone, and I wondered what this day would hold.

Thank goodness for the great directions Shohreh had given me. Of course I arrived just in time for the morning rush hour! I could handle anything after this!

West Isle is a quiet, beautiful, residential suburb of Mon-tréal with private homes and lawns rimmed in flowers. I soon found the address where Parvin lived and I must admit I was a little apprehensive as I rang the doorbell on the split-level home.

The door opened almost immediately. She must have been eagerly waiting for my arrival. Parvin rushed into my partially opened arms, burst into tears and sobbed. All I could say was, "Parvin, its OK." It seemed we stood as one for several minutes, this lady in black, filled with joy, yet deep in sorrow.

"Come, you must have something to drink and eat after such a long drive."

"It wasn't long. Only a little over an hour," I replied. However, I followed her up a flight of stairs into a cozy kitchen. "Really, Parvin, I am not hungry, but I sure could drink a cup of coffee." So our day began.

She could not leave the house since one of the children went to school for only a half a day with the other arriving at three. Our morning was spent with her taking me downstairs to her room, showing me the few personal keepsakes her mother had given her. Parvin's pain was evident as she told about her call to Iran that changed her life forever.

"They found my mother with the telephone receiver to her ear. She was trying to locate me to call me." I sat and just listened to her outpouring of pain. I soon realized she blamed herself, that she felt she should have been there with her mother. Oh, my dear Parvin! Your mother was so ill when you had to leave. I wanted to shout, "It was not your fault." Instead, I remained silent. Was this the time of cleansing, the beginning of healing? I hope so, my friend. I was moved to write these lines for her:

She was your beautiful rose
In your garden of flowers.
She enfolded you in her tender love,
Her kindness and gentleness
Were your nourishing nectar.
Still, she is the beautiful rose that blooms
In the heart of a loving daughter.

The children were lovely. A little girl and boy with black eyes and curly black hair. I could tell they were a handful, yet they respected Parvin.

Soon Shohreh and Jamshid arrived. I felt very welcomed in their home. Shohreh said, "Please, you will have dinner with us." It seemed I had just finished lunch, which was more like dinner as Parvin had prepared so many delicious dishes and served goodies all afternoon. "I would like to take Parvin out, Shohreh. Where is there a nice restaurant?" She recommended a large mall not far from her home. Parvin was taken by surprised when I told her we were going out. "I want to take you away from here just for a little while."

She hesitated, saying, "You can have dinner here." But I insisted. She had not gone anywhere since she had arrived many weeks ago.

I had no problem in finding the huge mall, but had to ask where we could find a restaurant. It was located in the upper level. As we began to eat, Parvin once again broke down. I quietly handed her a tissue, aware of eyes upon us. It did not bother me as I held her hand. No words were spoken; she knew I was there for her, as I would be in the coming months.

We shopped for more black blouses and skirts after dinner. It is the custom to wear black for forty days, but for Parvin it would be much longer.

A Friend Called Parvin

The building was large and cold
Made of metal and cement.
But holding with love
The frightened and unwanted
From around the world.

The many languages and cultures I behold
Wondering what way God would show,
I could make a difference, however small
To the many in this large hall.

Forlorn you sat—
Not wanting to be noticed in any way.
The hurt you brought from far away;
The sadness I saw in your eyes
Was all that you left across the sea.
Searching to find a better life
A strange land said,
"No, you must wait!"

So you wait and into my life you came
Like a soft breeze not to be seen.
But I saw and soon knew a friend so dear
That your tears are mine when turmoil appears.

So God showed me Parvin, my friend;
A small difference can be made
When I listen and understand your pain.

Our hands are joined, our hearts are filled
With love that grows
And no one can part what we have found
Those many months ago.

Fall, 1987

Thursday, September 24

This morning I would go to the bus station first, to wait
for the nine o'clock bus from Montréal. Faye, night supervi-

sor from the Salvation Army in Montréal, had called me last night, saying she was coming to spend the day. I greeted her with, "Hi, Faye, great to have you here. What would you like to do, go to the Salvation Army building, or ride with me?"

She replied, "I would like to ride with you for a while and see first-hand what your job entails, then spend time at the Army building. Fran, is this thing safe to drive?"

"Sure, you get use to the rattles and shakes," I said.

The morning went by quickly, doing the needed runs and discussing the program. Faye would see Darlene and Margot at lunchtime for any details she would like to know about. After lunch, Margot asked Faye if she would address the refugees in the chapel, going over what she thought would be important for them to know and what to expect once they were in Montréal. Faye went step-by-step over what the paralegals had already told them, but coming from someone involved with refugees in Montréal, they were reassured. She was asked many questions, answering all. "My advice: don't go out and buy $84.00 shoes with your first check. You, who are young and single, have to live on $180.00 per month. One young man bought shoes and was back to see me before half the month was over. You must be careful how you spend your money." (Father Martin had gone to see some of his boys in Montréal and found four or five of them sharing one apartment. Now I understood why.)

Rosemary had stopped in to see me just at the right time. Faye wanted to do some shopping before taking the evening bus back to Montréal. Rosemary offered to take her. Before I left I asked Faye for dinner. "I would love to, if it isn't any trouble for Rosemary to take me to your home." "No problem," was my friend's answer. John had the barbecue well underway when Faye arrived. She must have been many dollars poorer, judging by the packages she carried. However, she surprised me with gifts for Sue, Rosemary and me. They were soapstone figurines carved by an Eskimo artist named Wolf, from Canada. 'Course I got first choice!

Rosemary and I liked Faye from the moment we met her for the first time at the Salvation Army shelter in Montréal. She was friendly, had a great sense of humor and was a very caring person. This was a chance to ask her about her job. She proceeded to tell us about what her work entailed. The joy, the heartbreak of working with refugees in a large city. How innocent many were, while others were real conmen using the system. Pain clearly showed on her face as she told about a young Hispanic girl who had trusted a fellow countryman and how he had violated her. "I spent the whole night holding a weeping, child-like, young girl in my arms. I warn them, I talk about such things to the young women, but I failed to get through on this one." What a nightmare!

During the course of dinner she told me how impressed she was with the refugee program and the staff she had met today. She had seen the cooperation between the agencies and how smoothly things were run. I proudly replied, "We have a great staff that works together solving problems. And we still can laugh, not take things too seriously. It all seems to work out in the end."

"You are very fortunate, Fran, to work with such a team."

"Yes, I am the lucky one, Faye. I no longer take things for granted and realize how blessed I am to be American."

"I have more news," she announced. "I have accepted a new position with the Salvation Army in Cornwall, Ontario. I am very excited about it. I will be leaving in two weeks." I was surprised, but pleased for her. It meant a promotion and she would be back in her hometown.

Faye, you will be sorely missed in Montréal. I will always remember finding my car, late one night during a visit to the city, adorned with toilet paper, including and a big "bow" tied to the antenna. I then knew why Faye had disappeared after serving refreshments to Rosemary, Parvin and me, and then reappearing with a "Cheshire" grin. I would miss her.

Tuesday, October 6

There had been rumors off and on all summer that the Salvation Army had wanted to withdraw from the Refugee Program. Therefore it was not a surprise to the drivers when Margot informed us we would be moving from the Salvation Army building to the Dawn Motel the first week in October. Space had been made available for us in a large, glass-enclosed porch at the private residence of the motel owners, Tom and Nellie Routt. The one van, now being rented, would be left overnight at the motel with the keys placed in the mailbox for the driver working the following day. "Cookie," as manager Maria Pelkey was known, always had the names and room numbers of new arrivals, or knew if anyone had to see the nurse and had this information ready for the driver. She was the eyes and ears of the program at the motel. I looked forward to seeing Cookie with her sparkling eyes and bright smile. She had such a happy personality.

Pat and Paul Cote and I informed Margot we wanted to stay involved in the program since there would be fewer volunteer drivers needed with just the one van in use. We asked Margot to put our names at the top of the list.

The Cotes would work two days a week and I had three, with Sue doing lunch pickup on weekends. Other volunteers were on call to fill-in whenever needed

Barb Gilligan had taken a full time job as office assistant with Beekmantown School District. Rosemary McNamara took a position with the American Red Cross as their military representative on the air base. Kathy Champagne took a new position at Social Services. Rosemary and I continued to meet for coffee during the week and took trips together to Montréal.

Our friendship indeed had become close.

Darlene's clinic was moved to a room provided by Our Lady of Victory school, where health screenings, laundry facilities and lunch were all consolidated in one location. The arrangements for these facilities were made by Margot with Sister Theresa Martel, the executive director of Our Lady of Victory Secretarial School.

The hot lunches, I must say, were delicious. Everything was homemade by Beverly Frasier. She is the superb cook at the business school, excelling in everything from soup to her desserts that were everyone's weakness. Lloyd, on days it was served, somehow always got the last piece of homemade pie. (Darn!) If a refugee required a special diet, either for medical or religious beliefs, they received it now. It was no problem for Bev. Before returning to the motel, sandwiches with chips, fruit and a pint of milk were bagged by Bev and given to each refugee for their evening snack. A part-time cook was hired by Margot for weekend lunches, dinners and holiday breaks. On my first run to the motel, cereal, coffee and breakfast supplies were brought from Margot's storage at Catholic Charities and milk from Our Lady of Victory school where it was stored.

Lunch was a special time where Lloyd, Rolando (a paralegal) Margot and Darlene could sit together and go over any problems. More importantly, with fewer agencies involved it was a chance to discuss and give input for new ideas on how to improve the program. Responsibilities now fell on the shoulders of Social Services, Crisis Center, and Catholic Charities. That is to say, Lloyd worked under Director Brian Smith of the Crisis Center and Margot and Rolando under Director Denis Demers of Catholic Charities. Each worked independently, yet very closely with one another. The volunteers remained under the tender care of Margot.

Rose Pandozy, commissioner of Social Services, was

determined that any refugee stranded in Plattsburgh would not go hungry, would have proper shelter and clothing. She worked very hard toward that end in conjunction with the directors of the two other agencies.

Refugees (numbered about 85 in the area) who had or were able to obtain resources, rented small apartments or efficiency units at local motels.

Cash donations received at Catholic Charities from individuals, businesses and churches designated for the relief program were used for items that were not otherwise provided. Those items included medical bills, infant supplies and housing. Special dietary needs were met thanks to these donations, and the food boxes prepared by Joint Council of Economic Opportunity (JCEO), headed by Executive Director Conrad Kress, were supplemented with the additional funds. Drivers would pick up and deliver to the refugees the boxes prepared by JCEO employees David Hoy and Ed Annis. The food boxes contained canned vegetables, beans, tuna, soup, eggs, crackers, cheese, corn meal, rice, peanut butter, cereal, butter and bread. This was done without using any monies allocated for needy local residents.

For her part, Margot was desperately searching and applying for grants, since ten to thirty refugees continued to arrive each week. I wondered how long the refugee effort would survive.

Thursday, October 8

Religious services were looked forward to with much anticipation by these dispirited people. It was the one place where they felt safe in a world turned upside down.

The month of October is dedicated to the rosary. Father Martin, in his wisdom, combined the feast of "Our Lady of Guadalupe," December 12th, with the celebration of the rosary. Since Latin Americans recognize and honor this feast day it was Father's way for them to also honor the rosary. Our Lady of Guadalupe commemorates the appearance of the Holy Mother Mary appearing five times in 1531 A.D. to Juan Diego, a native American Indian, assuring him that she was indeed the Mother of God and that she would extend her protection to him. A shrine was built to commemorate these apparitions and is a place of pilgrimage. This is one of six apparitions of Mary around the world that has been approved by the Church and is recognized with feasts or celebrations.

I was asked by the women if I had time to take them to an inexpensive store where they could purchase material to make decorations. So off we went to K-Mart to the plastic flowers department. On the morning of the celebration, I took a van filled with women, men and children to Our Lady of Victory Church. I could feel the aura of excitement as they proudly carried their beautiful decorations. Under Father Martin's guidance, the men secured the four foot statue of the Virgin Mary to a platform that would be carried on shoulders in a solemn procession. Everyone took a turn carrying the statue, with the procession ending at the altar. Strong voices sang in unison as the children placed the homemade crown upon Mary's head. I was moved by the tears of reverence in their eyes. They were so far from home with a future unknown, but for a time in the house of God, they felt and were living their faith. Surely Our Lady of Guadalupe would extend her protection to them.

Wednesday, October 28

Joy, oh joy. Happy days are here again! We have a new van (well, almost new) a 1985 fifteen-passenger Dodge Ram. I knew Margot had been working intensely, searching so hard, these past months to replace the rental before winter came. When I reported to Catholic Charities on this crisp October morning, (drivers now reported directly to Margot), there, parked on the side-street, was this gorgeous van.

I practically flew up the stairs into Margot's office, finding this happy lady wearing a beautiful smile, pleased as punch. She had done what I was beginning to think was impossible. Not for this lady!

Now that I was in direct contact with Margot, we often had personal conversations before I left on my rounds. I found she thrived on challenges. Her compassion for the refugees was well known among other staff members and we, her volunteers, bathed in her loving, tender, care. Her concern in having a safe vehicle for transporting, which is the foundation of the program, was always uppermost in her mind. Now we had one, through the generosity of the Roman Catholic Diocese of Ogdensburg and their purchase of this van.

Margot had more news. With the Thanksgiving holiday approaching, the Salvation Army wanted to treat the refugees to a real holiday feast in the American tradition. The holiday spirit was very much alive and doing very well!

Friday, October 30

On my return trip from the Sundance Motel, after making food deliveries to refugees living there. I saw a Lebanese couple who had rented an apartment at Rip Van Winkle Motel walking and carrying their small child on North Margaret Street. Stopping, I asked, "Houssein, where are you going?" "To Our Lady of Victory school," he replied. "I am going that way," I said. "Come, I'll give you a ride." I was on my way to the Dawn for lunch pickup. I would just swing by the school first. "Are you going to see Darlene? Is something wrong with Mohammed?"

"No, we are going to a party." I knew of no party, but didn't question further.

On my return from the Dawn, I went into the OLV kitchen to help Bev serve lunch. There was giggling among the children, more than usual, it seemed, but I did not pay much attention. When I took my tray into the dining room, there sat Houssein and family, Margot, Darlene, Lloyd, Cookie, and Ginger and Nancy from the Salvation Army. With one voice they shouted "Happy Birthday." What a surprise! I almost spilled my soup. The children, one by one, handed me colored "Happy Birthday" drawings, each signed with their name and country. Houssein's wife, Hossan, handed me a small blue velvet case. Lifting the lid, I found an exquisite ivory necklace and brooch. I really did not want to take these keepsakes, but Hossan insisted with, "For all your kindness shown me and my family. We can never repay." Not wanting to offend her I accepted them, with many "shrowkranns" (thank yous).

Two Lebanese men who had just finished taking Mrs. Allen's French class appeared, handing me a slender, stem-like vase, holding a single rose. Lloyd disappeared, returning with a large decorated sheet cake. While doing the honors of cutting the cake, I asked, "Who knew and thought this up?" "Your friend Rosemary, but she could not come," Lloyd replied.

It was one of the best birthdays I had ever had, the first ever being encircled with radiating warmth from around the world as they sang "Happy Birthday" in Spanish, Arabic, and English.

Saturday, October 31

In midsummer there had been a cookout for the 25 to 30 refugees at a local park, but nothing since. With nothing to do or look forward to the days and nights were long.

With Halloween approaching, the students from Mrs. LaVarnway's psychology class at Our of Victory Secretarial School planned a lunchtime party for the refugee children with games and plenty of candy.

Our in-house resident artist, Meredith O'Connor, collected homemade goodies and organized an apple-dunking party with parents and children of both the refugees and volunteers participating. It was held on the 31st after lunch. Meredith appeared in the dining room, to the glee of the children, wearing a clown costume with a motley fuzzy wig and holding colorful balloons.

Meredith painted the children's faces and then the fun began. They were shown by Meredith how to bob for apples the American way. Towels were retrieved from the kitchen, for many children submerged their heads as well as their faces into the water for the elusive apples. Not to be denied, quick small hands captured their prize. Meredith and her husband Michael demonstrated a foot-stomping game with the goal being the breaking of balloons tied around their ankles. These children took it seriously! Many little bodies ended up on the floor, but oh, what bright smiles in the triumph of victory. However, they sure knew what to do with the "Pumpkin Piñata" that was filled with candy. With many "big league swings," children squealed in delight as they took turns trying to break it. Then they scrambled on the floor to gather the rewards!

This is what makes everything worthwhile, to see a parent smile, to hear the children's laughter.

Sunday, November 13

A phone call notified me of the expected schedule for Cora's operation for this coming Thursday. Earlier last month Cora had told me she had to undergo a serious operation. As we talked I felt how worried she was, not only about the operation, but also her family. I tried to reassure her by saying, "The medical facilities in Montréal are great," adding, "I will come to be with the girls and Oscar."

"It would mean a lot to me, Fran."

Thursday, November 19

Dawn was just breaking when I headed north. It was going to be a cold, beautiful day with no snow in the forecast. Thank goodness. I would first pick up Parvin, for she also wanted to be there. Of course I arrived in time for the morning rush hour over the Mercier Bridge, but after these many months I was used to it. No longer did I have a death grip on the wheel.

I had no problem finding the hospital, only in parking. We arrived just in time to see Cora before she was taken to the operating room. Then the awful waiting began. The small talk, the trips for another cup of coffee, the browsing in the gift shop, and then my buying a delicate violet plant in Cora's favorite color. Finally only silence as Oscar quietly paced the hall, then disappeared in search of news.

Rosemary once said, "Whenever I come here I feel I am entering another world." How true! The warmth of love made the hours seem like minutes as time evaporated in the company of these dear friends. And as I sat there deep in my thoughts, I remembered the wonderful dinners John and I had enjoyed in Montréal with these people. My semi-monthly trips with Rosemary where the fleeting hours were filled with laughter and music and, yes, even tears. Those special hours spent with Parvin into early morning made us realize how much more they all meant to us than just friends. For me they have become like members of my family. A bonding, from three points of the world, that forges strength. How rich I am!

Oscar reappeared, all smiles. A deep sigh of relief surged within me. I was allowed, under the pretense of being a family member, to see her for a few minutes. Wonderful, precious moments with good-bye hugs received and the ringing of "Thank you for coming," and "I will call you, Fran, tomorrow." I departed with Parvin. It was indeed a beautiful day!

Wednesday, December 16

I first saw this slender, attractive lady answering telephones at the Salvation Army building in March. I saw her again on moving day, from the National Guard building to the new shelter. She was driving the American Red Cross Disaster van, which was a disaster in itself. Rusted throughout, to the point it had holes in the floorboards and a rod where the gas pedal should be. Yet this daring lady transported refugees in it.

It wasn't until a few weeks later when I came on duty at 6:30 a.m. that I met her. "Hi, I am Sister Monique," she said. "I've seen you around." What a surprise! I had not realized upon first meeting her that she was a nun, except that she wore a crucifix symbolizing her faith. Sister was so energetic and warm, a let's-get-it-done, caring person, dressed comfortably in a blouse and slacks. She continued, "I come as often as I can at 5:00 or 5:30 in the morning and stay until 7:30 a.m., that is, when I have time and I am in town." I learned from Margot that Sister Monique was the regional director of the Department of Christian Formation (at Plattsburgh) for the Diocese of Ogdensburg.

I remember seeing cases of sample bars of soap, shampoo, towels and personal items, miraculously appearing in the storage room of the shelter. My curiosity got the better of me and I asked Captain Champlin. They had been brought in by Sister Monique. It was like manna from heaven.

After the shelter closed it was not an end to the need for basic necessities. An additional demand for sheets and bedding existed because of the rental of apartments by refugees, a task that Sister seemed to take on personally. Soon Margot's storage shelves in the Catholic Charities garage, which Ray Peterson (a volunteer) had built, were overflowing with bedding. She did not stop there but also collected the much-needed pots and pans. I am sure I am not aware of many other items she labored to obtain.

Sister traveled all over the northeast with contacts ranging from New Hampshire to Vermont and Northern New York. She never forgot or hesitated to ask assistance of hospitals, hotels or convents on behalf of her refugees even to this day. I remembered, especially, the elderly nuns at Sister Monique's Provincial House in Littleton, N.H., who spent months knitting hats, slippers, mittens and booties for the oncoming winter. On their arrival they were quickly given out. However, so many had been made they would also be given as gifts at our refugee Christmas party.

Sister Monique, you are truly a caring, giving, special lady.

Saturday, December 19

A monthly newsletter called the *Refugee Relief Effort*, under the auspices of Catholic Charities and the Plattsburgh Interfaith Council, was written by the volunteer coordinator. Starting in February 1987, it was mailed to nearly 300 volunteers listed in the volunteer's register and to others who had a bona fide interest in the refugee relief program.

In Margot's December newsletter a call had gone out for baked goods, toys and small personal items to make gifts for the Christmas refugee party. It was to be held in the evening in the conference room at Our Lady of Victory school.

Meredith O'Connor solicited gifts, both for children and adults, from generous local businesses: Meyer's Pharmacy, Rams Department Store, and Toys for Joy. In addition, Meredith's friends gave her a cash donation to buy added gifts.

Earlier today as I looked out the window, snow was still falling. It was supposed to cease by nightfall. I sure hoped so, for tonight I would attend the refugee party at Our Lady of

Beta, a child of Afghanistan.

Victory and tomorrow John and I would be going to Montréal to celebrate an early Christmas dinner with Maritza and Percy. We then would go on to Oscar's, where Parvin would join us.

Bowls of fruit, one for Maritza and Percy, the other for Oscar and family, were made ready earlier today. The gifts for Maria, Erika and Sandra were being wrapped by John as I finished the final decorations on our tree. Our car trunk would be full. On returning this mid-morning, we found a large bagful of brightly wrapped gifts on our doorstep labeled for Oscar's family with no note as to who might have left it. I suspected Sue Steuart, for she knew we were going Saturday. It proved to be true.

On this anticipated evening I brought a car full of excited children and parents to Our Lady of Victory. The rest of the forty or fifty refugees would be brought by van and in other private cars.

The chatter of voices led us to a large room with a

garnished fireplace, beset by piles of colorful wrapped gifts, and rows of chairs lining the walls. Off at one end of the room was the long row of decorated tables laden with an array of baked goods and glass bowls of punch. Many former volunteers from the shelter were in attendance. It would be a night for reminiscing, a time to celebrate together once again.

From the Middle East, Eastern Africa, South America, Central America, and North America it was an international celebration with everyone partaking of food and drink side by side. There was no disparity of religion shown in the gathering of Moslems and Christians this special evening, although I must say, the Moslems from Africa had bewilderment in their eyes. They really didn't know what to make of all this, especially when, a "Ho-Ho-Ho" Santa appeared. Some children drew a little closer to their parents while others squealed in delight.

Margot was Santa's helper and she soon had Santa encircled with the many sitting children from the different nations. As Santa (Ron Wood) played his mandolin and sang familiar Christmas songs he was soon joined in many languages as eyes in little black faces stared in awe of him. Oh, how the eyes lit up when their name was called for their gift. Their shyness soon disappeared as they marveled at the merriment of other children and in watching a game that I am sure did not make sense to them, the breaking of the Christmas Piñata. And there was joy and peace this night.

Special Season

A celebration is about to begin,
Joy and rejoicing are at hand.
Time to spend with family and friends
Knowing the warmth of love.

I am blessed with support from loved ones near
Who saw and understood
Time given to those in need

As they fled from fear.

The unwanted that passed this way
Leaving families and homes far away.
May this special season bring
Peace and happiness once again.

Let this joyful season begin
Renewal of hope and love
To mankind.
Then the world will know
"Peace on earth, good will to men."

Winter, 1987

Sunday, December 20

The morning greeted us with overcast skies in a winter wonderland. The road crews had done a super job on the Northway and the auto-route in Canada. John and I enjoyed the winter scenery of snow-laden trees, the coverlet of white on sleeping meadows creating a pristine freshness over the landscape.

When we arrived in Montréal we found the side street where Maritza lived still unplowed. We walked several blocks through five inches of fluffy snow and hoped the wind wouldn't rise before returning home tonight or then our stay in the city would be extended.

"Merry Christmas, Maritza. How do you like all this snow?" "I no like. It is so cold," but our embraces were warm as was our welcome to the sparsely furnished apartment. Wonderful aromas floated from the kitchen. John and I were more then ready to feast on the South American dinner. With the lifting of glasses in a toast for health and happiness in the coming new year, John and I sat down to a banquet of specially prepared holiday dishes. I cannot recall the name of even one dish, but all were wonderful.

"How is Ryan and Brendan? Chris and Mike?," Maritza asked as she handed me a large envelope holding pictures of her young Laura. "Fine," I replied. My heart filled, knowing John and I would spend our Christmas with our loved ones.

Percy said, "We are thinking of going to Toronto." My heart leaped! He went on to say how hard it was here with just factory work for him and part-time work at Harvey's Restaurant for Maritza. They felt they were looked down on because they weren't fluent in French, although both had taken the amount of free classes allowed by the government. He continued, "It is so hard. We must find better jobs and in Toronto, it's English-speaking, with better opportunities. I want to bring my parents with Laura, as soon as we receive our immigrant papers." It had been almost a year and a half for Percy; still he had not heard anything from Ottawa. How lives are played with, it seems. Then it was time to leave for Oscar's.

"Merry Christmas" resounded at Oscar's as John and I went to each and every one, receiving a warm hug and kiss. A beautifully decorated tree, embellished with miniature lights, was the bright focal point in an otherwise drab living room. Cora told us "Sue came last week to see me, bringing a complete dinner and the artificial tree with decorations. It seems a little like Christmas, especially with you and Mr. John now here."

Our afternoon began with Oscar and Maria conversing with John in the living room and I with Cora in the kitchen. Erika and Sandra divided their time between both rooms, eyeing the gifts that surrounded the symbol of our holiday season.

The knock on the door announced the awaited arrival of Parvin. Bundled against the cold, her face was flushed from the bite of the brisk, cold mid-day. She stepped into waiting arms, glowing with happiness. Her laughter filled the small room. It had been so long since I had seen her radiant smile and heard her gleeful laughter. The wonderful, warm gathering of dear friends was now complete.

As the afternoon slipped by, we took in the joy of being with one another, and listened to their hopes and their dreams for the new year. Parvin, now ready to find an apartment in the city, seemed anxious to get on with her life. Oscar had submitted resumes to companies in his field in hopes for a call that would bring an interview. Maria, working as an assistant manager at a large supermarket, hoped to apply to a college in the coming year. Erika and Sandra were still adjusting to school. Cora was recovering day by day from her operation. Hope is what our dreams are made of.

The City Of Lights

Across the bridge I traveled
Into the City of Lights
That embraces
The despairing people of the world.

I step into arms of love
That radiate beyond the cold,
And I thank God
For these friends that passed my way.

Laughter fills the air,
Quiet words spoken,
Touching of hands across the table,
Reassurance I am near.

Day ends, night falls,
And I leave the City of Lights
In wonderment
Of love I felt this day.

Tuesday, February 16

During the Christmas holidays just one couple from Lebanon came to the empty Dawn Motel. Everyone else had gone to Canada. Sue, who was volunteering, brought them home to spend the day with her and her family.

When I came on duty a few days before the New Year, I heard about this couple's tragic journey from Margot. I was to deliver their food with other food boxes to the Sundance where they were renting.

Although I had every intention of not becoming personally involved with any more refugees, I found myself, once again, drawn to this couple, perhaps because they were from the Middle East, a part of the world that fascinated me. I had learned and began to understand so much more over these past months that could never be taught in a history class or the media. The personal experiences of meeting and communicating on a one-to-one basis made it easy.

They were a lovely couple though filled with torment by the death of their eleven year old daughter from cancer just two days before Christmas at Saint Jude's Children Hospital in Memphis, Tennessee.

Their pain showed and I soon found myself stopping in to see them even when duty did not call to do so. My instinct was to respond in some way to this couple, who found themselves in a strange land and in so much pain, if only to listen.

We talked while having coffee and Peg and Tony's tragic story slowly unfolded. "She was our only daughter, the youngest of three. Her cancer had been in remission for a year, until two months ago." Tony had to stop as he tried unsuccessfully to silence the sobs that racked him. My hand touched his ever so lightly across the table. Peg continued with tears in her eyes, "The doctors did not have the necessary medicine or equipment in Lebanon to treat her." Her face drawn by the strain of tightly holding in her emotions, she went on, "We had two choices. We could go to France or come to the United

States. Time was of the essence and our greatest enemy. We had our visas for the States, so we chose the highly recommended Saint Jude's Children Hospital." And I thought, what a heinous disease, especially when it hits your child!

Peg and Tony are Christians. They had to go through Syrian-held lines to get to the airport. They knew the President of Lebanon on a personal basis, as well as Ambassador Kelly of the United States. I did not know our Ambassador was still there. Arrangements were made to let the Red Cresent (Red Cross) ambulance through under escort, leaving their two teenage sons behind.

They spent anguished weeks as doctors fought a losing battle, and faced the irony of being told if their daughter had been brought when the disease first appeared, they felt confident they could have cured her, because of the type of cancer, leukemia. Again Tony broke down. I wondered, "What am I doing here! Putting myself through this. Is it the humane feelings, stirring deep within, that I can't deny toward my fellow man? Yes, I cannot turn away."

Still, there were good memories they would never forget. The doctor who hosted them at his home for Thanksgiving dinner. The nurses and staff members who gave their support, showering them with kindness, and at the end, many accompanying them to the funeral. Finally she was at rest, at peace.

Peg and Tony had a hearing date in late February. The wait of entry was getting longer. Over the following weeks their pain seemed to ease. Their loss, their hurt would be with them forever. John met them and he would stop with me to have coffee with them. One day, as we were speaking about Lebanon and the many ethnic groups of people, Tony said, "We are Phoenician." Without a thought I blurted out, "I thought you all went the way of the dinosaurs!" Peg and Tony burst out laughing. It was wonderful.

Again calls were made to Lebanon to the proper people in power. They were desperate to get their sons Mark and Karl out, but they didn't have visas. Finally Ambassador Kelly issued them. Escorted to the airport, the boys flew from Beirut to New York City, where anxious parents waited just two days before their hearing date.

All their power, their wealth, or who they knew could not prevent the loss of their country or their most precious gift, their beloved daughter. I wish them well, Mark, Karl, Peg and Tony, in their quest for a new life in Canada.

Peg had told Sue Steuart that they dressed their little girl in a white dress for burial, for she would never be a bride. When Sue drove to Texas for her own daughter's wedding, she returned by Memphis, Tennessee, stopping, searching and finding the little girl's resting place. Sue placed her daughter's bridal bouquet on the grave, a heart-rending touch.

Wednesday, February 17

The program that everyone had thought would end in June of last year continued into 1988 with renewed vigor. There were 58 refugees in our area, 8 temporarily living at the Dawn Motel, 34 supporting themselves locally, and 15 in host homes. Canadian law had not changed. The people seeking refugee status were still being welcomed across the border.

The Refugee Relief Effort was still being covered by television stations from both sides of the border, praising the effort of the community. The *National Geographic* magazine found the story of Plattsburgh and its volunteers an interesting part of their coverage on Canadian-American border relations and mentioned it in their article on the subject.

Still, Social Services oversaw the Refugee Program with Crisis Center and Catholic Charities doing the day-to-day relief effort, while Plattsburgh Interfaith Council continued its support with the hiring of a paralegal advisor, Rolando

Miranda. Rolando had been a volunteer paralegal for many months. The Joint Council of Economic Opportunity and the Salvation Army provided support for those in the area who needed food or clothing.

These are excerpts from Margot's monthly newsletter in the early months of the new year. We saw 1082 refugees pass through Plattsburgh in 1987. We suspect there will be a greater flow of refugees into Plattsburgh with the United States Employer Sanctions going into effect this past May and to be stringently enforced in the coming year. The past summer of 1987 will also be remembered with the visit and celebration of Mass by Archbishop Vargas of Peru, South America, at Saint Augustine's Church in Peru, New York.

Br-r-r-r Twenty Below

To start the van
On a cold arctic morn
Takes pumping of foot
And quick of hand.

The sputtering motor
Finally starts
Engulfed in vapor
And frozen words.

Squeaking of tires
On surface so slick
Around corners is
A neat trick.

On rounds we go
Doing our duty
For those who wished
They were in Miami.

And we settled in against the North Country winter.

Friday, March 11

It is very unusual to have a young girl, even at the age of

twenty, travel alone, unescorted, from foreign countries. But this was not the case for Jamie from Lebanon, who arrived mid-February.

I met her at the Crisis Center, a vibrant, bright young lady who spoke two languages and English fairly well. By afternoon she was settled in at the Sundance Motel with the many other refugees renting there. Jamie had rented an apartment by herself, which concerned Margot, for she would be living alone for the next three weeks. Although Peg and Tony were still there to watch over her, they would be leaving in the next few days. So here I went again, but not alone. Winnie and Sandy Armstrong, owners of Sundance, took Jamie under their wing. I made a point of stopping every day, sometimes going back in the evening to spend time with her. I told her not to open the door to anyone, unless she knew who they were. Especially not to open the door to any refugee man, even if he used the pretext that he needed to borrow a can opener. I said, "Tell them to see Winnie." At that time there were a lot of young single men at the motel.

John and I would pick Jamie up for Sunday Mass, then go to a local restaurant for breakfast, bringing her home to spend part of the day afterwards. She found our winter so cold. Even bundled, her face and hands would become swollen. I told Jamie, "Just a few weeks ago, I picked up a family from Central America. The woman and her children had no socks, wearing just slippers and lightweight clothing. This is why there is a box full of heavy sweaters, all sizes, on the van. I called Margot from the motel telling her about them. Margot met me at the Crisis Center with children's and women's boots, which weren't the best looking, but they served the purpose. I took them directly from the Crisis Center to Catholic Charities' garage for coats. We drivers see this all the time." I added that a Somalian man had asked me, "Is it true it gets so cold that your nose will freeze and fall off?" I had been driving the van when his question took me completely

121

by surprise. He was so serious, I had to stifle myself from bursting out in laughter. I explained to this man, who came from a country where one hundred degrees is cool, the North Country winter code. "You wear layers of warm clothing, warm coat, hat, warm socks and boots, then a scarf across your face with only your eyes showing." "Oh Fran, this is not true, is it?" "It saves your nose, Jamie!" I replied.

"Jamie, how come you are traveling by yourself?" She proceeded to tell me, "My mother knew there was no future any longer in Lebanon for me. She insisted I come." She explained further that she had been a second year university student, majoring in archaeology with a minor in Assyrian language. Her father's heart was broken when plans were made for her to travel with a friend of the family to Ohio, where she had an uncle. Upon her visa's expiration, she made plans to go to Montréal, where she had relatives. An uncle owned a restaurant there. She would be able to work for him. "But I enjoy it here. I am becoming responsible and independent. Before, my father took care of everything. Even small problems. I am growing up."

Her father would follow later in the spring, she hoped, with her mother and two sisters coming perhaps in the summer. Many things had to be taken care of at home first. It takes a lot of money to come, and furniture and other personal possessions would have to be sold. Inflation in Lebanon is so high they would not receive a very good price for the items. "It is so hard," a sad Jamie replied.

John and I decided to take Jamie, with our oldest grandson Brendan, to the Winter Carnival in Saranac Lake. Chris, Mike and Ryan would join us later at the Hotel Saranac for dinner.

If Jamie thought Plattsburgh was cold, she stepped into an "ice box" in Saranac Lake! It was a beautiful, cold, clear day where "Sun-Dogs" (reflection of the sun's rays from the vertical faces of ice prisms in the atmosphere) played in a sky of icy-blue. It was a day on which you didn't just stand around!

She could not believe the castle was made from blocks of ice. As Jamie walked with us through it, stopping to admire the beautiful ice sculptures, we noticed her reaching out, touching, feeling the shimmering wall that glittered bluish green. "It is so beautiful. I can't believe it is ice."

Brendan asked, "Gramie, will you take me down the slide?" "No, Brendan. That's for your dad to do." Besides, I was cold enough. We strolled around as squeals filled the crystal air from children on their wild ride down the icy run. It was getting late. It was time for us to go to the hotel.

We made our way upstairs to a large room where a huge fireplace sent out warmth. There were two long leather couches, separated by an enormous wooden coffee table, all positioned next to the dancing flames. The room held tables and chairs, and there was a piano at each end. Our attention was drawn to an old-fashioned counter attended by a man with a pigeonhole cabinet behind him.

As we sat, sipping refreshing beverages, taking in the warmth of the fire, thoroughly enjoying the quaint surroundings of this old hotel, Jamie asked, "Do you think I may play the piano?" I didn't know this young lady could play piano! "I can ask the man at the desk." Within moments the room resounded with classical music. Her talent showed as she played one piece after another, all from memory. People were stopping to listen. I snuggled a little deeper into the leather softness of the couch, feeling the beautiful sound filling my senses. And all was right with the world this evening.

Chris, Mike and Ryan arrived in the middle of her performance, joining us in the pleasure of this personal recital. They had not met Jamie before, but since Mike is an artist in her own right, it was not long before the two were taken with one another. All too soon it was time to go in to a scrumptious dinner. What a wonderful ending to a beautiful day.

John and I took Jamie to the border on her entry date. Relatives would come down from Montréal to pick her up at the border. While waiting to be called for her short interview, she said, "This is worse than going to the dentist." I broke up with laughter.

As she was getting ready to leave with her relatives, I asked, "Do you have Parvin's telephone number?"

"Yes," she said.

I told her, "I called Parvin last night again and she will be down to see you at the Hotel Europa. If you need her call her."

"I will. Thank you both for everything." With a mixture of smiles and tears came a last embrace before she left for the "City of Lights."

Spring, 1988

Saturday, April 9

John and I had moved Parvin early in the new year. We had taken furniture with us to help furnish her new apartment. We did not know that mattresses, unless new (which they were but with the protective plastic removed), could not be taken into Canada unless for a relative. We didn't want to pay the Canadian duty tax on a new mattress, so that is why the plastic had been removed. At the Canadian border, the customs officer said, "The rest of the furniture is fine, but the mattresses you cannot take in unless they are for a relative."

I kept repeating, "It is for a friend." Three times the officer asked, "They aren't for a relative?" Finally it dawned on me. John and I left to go through another Port of Entry.

This time when asked, I said, "For my son at McGill University." "Go ahead." Stephen had been an exchange student there a few years ago.

Rosemary and I looked forward to our semi-monthly visits, while John and I went monthly to the north. Rosemary and I spent most of our time with Parvin in her apartment in the city, which she shared with Aram, sister of Lila. Aram was in a Master's Degree Program at McGill University.

The day seemed to slip by in quiet conversation about her life or listening to music from her country as she sang along in her lovely voice. The haunting songs lingered in one's mind. We explored the great city, Montréal, then returned to feast on a banquet of Iranian dishes (a favorite, Ghormeh Sabzi Polo, is a meat dish served with rice) where words became lost in our laughter. The evening succumbing to night, she spoke of her hope of being accepted into the French class, a seven month program. In the meantime, she paid for and had attended a four week English class at McGill University. Parvin told us of the fear and terror she felt for her uncle and his family in Tehran now that Iraq was capable of sending and hitting that city and others with missiles. This uncle was like a father to Parvin. As the night waned, giving way to the hours of early morn, Rosemary and I lingered in our good-byes, never expecting Parvin's greatest fear might come true!

Wednesday, April 13

Her elegant attire spoke of European fashion—this Yugoslavian lady who was married to a Lebanese man for twenty some years. She was fluent in four languages, as were her two teen-age daughters, Alice and Merei.

Like others, Sonia expected to go right through to Montréal where her husband Robert waited. He had gone to Canada, but not through Plattsburgh, eight months before. Sonia's disappointment in having to stay here for four weeks

A family of Lebanon with author to be brought to Health
Screening. Sundance Motel. 1988.

turned into a positive experience with her and the girls taking
an active part in the relief program.

Each day Alice would work in the nurse's clinic helping
Darlene as a translator or taking general health notes in the
screenings. Alice's ability as a linguist proved to be highly
beneficial when a Somalian woman needed kidney dialysis.
The daughter of the Somalian woman knew Arabic. They
were able to communicate from Somalian to Arabic through
Alice and to English for the necessary medical information.

Merei gave her time as a translator for Rolando in his
paralegal work. Sonia, always ready to help, would ride with
me at times in delivering food boxes. She would translate
from Arabic to English any problems that would arise.

Sonia had helped her people who came under attack in
her country. She was a very courageous lady. Although she
was Christian, it did not matter when sheets from her own bed
were needed for bandages in binding the wounds of either
Christians or Moslems. She also transported them to the
hospital. "We are all human beings no matter what our
belief," she would often say.

In spite of the danger, she felt on one occasion she was really going to die. Sonia was returning to her home and along the way she had to pass through several road blocks (checkpoints) held by opposing factions. The last blockade before entering into a safe zone which was several hundred feet away was unguarded, so she continued on. Sonia heard the sound of a gun being cocked. In her rear view mirror she saw a teenage boy aiming his rifle at her. Pushing the accelerator, down she made it to safety. "I thought, Fran, I was going to be shot. Why he didn't, I don't know." Once settled in at the Sundance she became very depressed with the waiting and her surroundings. "I never lived like this," she told me on one of my many visits. On the other hand, Alice and Merei were finding joy in their freedom, to the dismay, at times, of their mother. Sonia was ready to call me the day the two girls were gone for two hours, unescorted in a strange country. They had found the small shopping plaza ten minutes from the Sundance, and with window shopping time was forgotten. The worst of times was the day two U.S. Border Patrolmen barged through Sonia's opened door, with a startled Alice being told to wait outside. They asked in military fashion, for papers. Sonia responded, "Which papers? Yugoslavian passport, Lebanese passport, American visa or my papers for entry into Canada?"

"We'll ask you for what we want," was the rough reply. It was right out of a "Western" TV script. She told me later, "I was so frightened."

The last Sunday they were here, John and I took them out for breakfast, then a ride to AuSable Chasm and on to Lake Placid. We stopped to stroll the narrow streets and had coffee in a quaint restaurant overlooking Mirror Lake. They loved it.

On their entry date, John decided to take the day off so we could take them in his pick-up truck to Robert. Alice and

Merei thought it was a ball to ride in the back with the many suitcases. Though it was mid-April it was still quite cool. I gave the girls a wool blanket to keep warm. However, they were so excited about seeing their father after these many months, they never used it.

"It is so cold, Fran," Sonia said.

"Spring is coming, Sonia."

This dear family became very close to us but they would be the last that I became emotionally involved with, for I no longer wanted to lose a bit of my heart.

Sonia and Robert, indeed we felt the warmth of spring each time we sat at your table.

The Journey

Months of terror and loneliness
You left across the sea,
Seeking once more
A family to be.

So close you came
To your dream,
Only to be delayed
By a law unforeseen.

A heart in despair,
Tears that flowed unseen,
You drew on waning strength
To accept what cannot be.

I was a stranger
Who held out a hand,
For you to grasp
And become a friend.

Now the waiting is passed
And you will leave,
For the loved one
No longer out of reach.

Saturday, April 16

"I would be friends with you and have your love."

William Shakespeare

Their unconditional love, Maritza and Percy, Oscar and family, and Parvin, showed in many ways. The personalized holiday cards John and I received, including one from Parvin. The special Valentine card from Maria that begins, "To My Dear Parents," with a short message that touched our hearts deeply. The dinners, the telephone calls to us, our welcome as overnight guests at Cora and Oscar's, the first time Rosemary and I attended the wonderful, so different, Iranian concert as guests of Parvin, taking delight in seeing Akbar again and meeting Parvin's other friends, especially Mehri.

Yet, it was a very difficult time for them. Erika wanted to go home, causing great distress not only for Oscar and Cora, but to Sandra and Maria. Oscar, in not receiving any calls for interviews, would now pay to take a course in real estate. Until they received their landed immigrant papers, doors would not open under their present status unless they wanted to work in a factory, which Oscar and Cora did for a time. By taking and passing the real estate exam, he hoped to stand and go forward on his own abilities.

Parvin had been accepted into the French program. She was very hopeful as to what the coming months would bring. Aram, her roommate, had to withdraw from the university to undergo open heart surgery in Ottawa at age 28. This brought a new roommate, Sussan. She was the niece of Ali, who managed the intimate, small Iranian cafe where Rosemary, Parvin, and I, and yes, even John, enjoyed warm hospitality. It was there that John and I were offered, by an older Iranian man (a stranger, but known by Parvin and Ali) to stay at his home overnight. "Arrangements have been made to stay with other friends," we explained to Ali, "but thank him very much. He is very kind to offer." We were never allowed to pay for coffee when we stopped in.

Monday, April 18

Parvin's collect call came late evening. She was very upset and was calling from a pay phone, which surprised me, for she had a telephone. She was crying, saying something had been taken from her. My heart sank, thinking the worst. "Are you hurt?"

"No, Fran. All my jewelry, my mother's keepsakes that I had hidden in my suitcase under packed clothes, were taken from the closet. Nothing else. My heart is on fire again." I told her Rosemary and I were planning to go to see her this weekend. "I will be waiting for you, Fran," she said.

We learned on our arrival that only Parvin's jewelry was taken. The clothes were not disturbed, nor were there signs of forced entry. Since renovations were being made on their floor, Parvin and Sussan could easily be watched whenever they came or went. The workmen had pass keys but it would be impossible to prove they were involved, so it was never reported to the police. Instead they moved to a new location in another part of the city.

Saturday, April 23

Shortly after moving into their new apartment, Rosemary and I went to spend the day with Parvin. She was very subdued in her greeting, wearing black again. I looked at Rosemary, Rosemary looked at me, however we did not say anything until she went into another room. Rosemary asked Sussan, "Why is Parvin wearing black?"

"She received a call late yesterday from Iran that her uncle died."

"The uncle she thinks of as a father?" I asked in shock.

"No, another uncle in her hometown of Shiraz. He died in a missile attack." Oh God!

When Parvin returned, we told her how sorry we were. The words seemed so inadequate, as she sat down between Rosemary and I on the sofa. We proceeded to look at the photos I had brought, taken from an earlier visit. No tears, no outburst, very unusual. The day was spent quietly.

That evening I was sitting on the floor with her, giving her copies of photos she wanted. It seemed inappropriate to do so earlier. Soft Iranian music played in the background as Rosemary and Sussan looked on. With a rush, Persian words poured forth as she burst into tears. Taken by surprise, I inched back from her. Sussan intently watched and listened as tears streamed down her face. Feeling Parvin's pain, I put my arms around her, rocking back and forth, speaking quietly, feeling her spirit being drained. God, help her! When is it ever going to get better?

Haven

So unjust
Life can be,
Strife with no end
It seems.

Crimes against the heart
Continually come your way,
Piercing arrows
Bleeding strength away.

Come my friend
To the shelter of love,
Recline your head
On my shoulder.

A haven
For your heart to mend,
Find refuge in my strength
And restore your soul.

Tuesday, April 26

"If we were to drive down Sainte-Catherine Street in Montréal with a banner emblazoned with Plattsburgh, N.Y., we would be overwhelmed," I said to Lloyd one day in early spring. "Then let's have a reunion!" he replied.

The volunteers, as well as staff, wondered about the thousands that had passed our way. Except for the few that had formed close friendships, we did not know how the others were or how they were doing. I thought it was a great idea but never expected it to go anywhere.

Thursday, April 27

"Hi girl! Got a new job for you," was my greeting from Margot on my arriving early one morning in late April.

"And what might that be?"

"Plans for a reunion in Montréal," she replied with a bright smile.

"All right!!"

Margot had had occasion to speak with Ron Wood about the reunion. He thought it was a marvelous idea. He told her the Plattsburgh Kiwanis Club, of which he was a member, might be interested in co-sponsoring it with the Montréal Kiwanis. He would work on it. She went on, "We need someone, some organization, to help formulate plans on that end. We need to find a large enough place to hold the reunion that will be easy for everyone to get to, as well as a place with cover in case it rains. They would know."

She wanted me to contact those I knew to help get the news out to others in Montréal. "Ok, I'll contact Sue to get the telephone number of her Somalian friend Abdullah, and Nancy Tyrell's Sri Lankan friend, Sugmar. I'll call Oscar, Sonia and Parvin. If they agree, we'll have our group ready,"

I said.

Friday, May 28

Our son Stephen and his wife Mary Lee arrived for a visit over Memorial Day weekend. They came at a time when the annual Benson and Hedges International Fireworks competition was taking place in Montréal. (We had gone with Chris and family last year to Cora and Oscar's home to enjoy this spectacular show.) On learning there would be competition tonight they wanted to go.

After a hasty call had been made to a surprised but happy Cora we were on our way north. It would be just a short walk from Cora's home to the Jacques Cartier bridge where we would have a fantastic view, as the bridge is closed to traffic and thousands of people have a grandstand view from here.

It was an evening of sharing not only the beautiful spectrum of the night but the joy of these special friends in meeting the rest of our family. Truly the warm arms of hospitality were felt once again in the "City of Lights."

It was quite late as the last cups of refreshments were being consumed and we offered Parvin a ride home. It would not be out of our way. Stephen, Mary Lee, and Parvin conversed easily with one another as John drove leisurely through this beautiful city, captivating us in the night with its lights. I saw Parvin was completely at ease with Stephen and Mary Lee, as she had been with Chris and Mike. They in turn were charmed by her demure personality and I felt her drawing closer to our family.

Saturday, June 11

Margot, Meredith O'Connor and I rode with Ron Wood to Montréal to have lunch as guests of the Saint George Kiwanis Club at the Montréal Athletic Club on Peel Street. After a wonderful luncheon, a meeting was held with Jack

LeClair, the president of the club, and Rev. Don Gibson, who had agreed to head the committee to work with us.

Summer, 1988

Saturday, June 25

Margot and I returned for another meeting. This time it was held in a cozy room at the Mont Royal United Church where Rev. Gibson was pastor in Ville Mont Royal. Robert and family, Oscar, Cora, and Parvin were already there waiting for us, as was Jack LeClair and several other committee members. We were being introduced to Rev. Gibson's "right-hand man," Leroy, and other committee members as Abdullah walked in. The meeting began with Rev. Gibson recommending the large park near the church, since the particular facility at the Olympic Stadium they had looked into was being used. This park had a large building with a recreational room with plenty of chairs and tables in case it rained.

At this time it was estimated between 250 to 500 might attend. Everyone would be told to bring his own food, with soda being supplied by the Kiwanis Clubs. Oscar said, "Many are having a hard time right now. They might not have the food for the picnic." It was suggested when calls were made that extra food be made for one additional person. Robert said, "My family will bring extra. But my concern is the distance people will have to travel here. It involves going to the end of the Metro line and then taking a bus." In the end it was still decided this would be the best location.

Tuesday, June 28

June had been a very busy month for volunteering as well as family life. Summer was coming into its own with a forecast for a hot July.

Rosemary and I had continued to see Parvin over the past weeks and I asked her on this visit if she would be free for a weekend in July. I felt the need to have a mini-weekend away from demanding obligations.

Saturday, July 9

The weekend agreed upon turned out to be hot and humid, with temperatures in the high nineties, a perfect time to leave the sticky city of Montréal. This would be our first time spent together over an extended period other than just for a day. I was looking forward to not only to getting away, but to taking Parvin on a break from her French studies and enjoying scenery away from the city.

After taking in the Granby Zoo, I drove to a small village located near the Richelieu River and found a motel near a large park, a lovely location with friendly people. It was here in this picturesque setting that my Western mind was intro- duced to Eastern beliefs and culture. The hours spent in sharing brought with them a knowledge of a world that was so foreign to me. My door of curiosity opened wider to her light. As I listened I began to understand why this sensitive lady had inspired my humble poetry.

The rest of that afternoon was spent beside the locks, watching pleasure boats of all sizes going through. Parvin was fascinated by the operation, and in my non-mechanical way I tried to explain how they worked. She seemed to understand.

That evening, after dining on French cuisine, classical music softly filled our room from her cassette player. She loved classical music, from Tchaikovsky to Mozart; the great painters, from Van Gogh to Picasso; great writers, from Shakespeare to Robert Frost; and to my surprise, many west- ern pop singers, especially Barbra Streisand.

Time slipped by unnoticed as I learned about a world that I felt was so mysterious, with questions being answered graciously by Parvin. Particularly of interest to me was the respect I had witnessed, and admired, that was given in their greetings to their elderly.

"We honor them for the wisdom and knowledge of life they hold," she softly replied. She continued about how children looked after their parents or elderly relatives, not only out of duty, but for the love and respect held for them. She told me that grandmothers and mothers are especially honored for the sacrifices they have given for the family. Then I was asked, in turn, about nursing homes that she had seen and read about. "Why is this?" she asked, as I grimaced inside.

I dwelt on the reasons, or were they excuses, for today's western ways and complexities as she sat with a quizzical expression. Finally I ended with, "It has not always been this way, Parvin. In past years the elderly were treated much the same way as they are in your world." Why did I feel a stirring of shame?

I turned my evening of enlightenment to, and we discussed at length, what I considered a parable for humility which a young Iranian man had told me:

> It is like a tree. To be too straight is to break.
> To bend is being able to yield, and yet, have strength.
> To bow deeply is to lower oneself, showing weakness.

Searching a little deeper I asked Parvin, if I were to offend her, would she let me know? (The young man had said, "No. Your friend would not." Then how would I know, I had thought.) I said it would be done through my being uninformed in Eastern customs, and not with malice. Parvin looked at me and smiled. I then knew I would have to wait for another time, another day for my answer. And as the night waned, we realized our values and beliefs were not very different, that we had much in common.

The next day I attended services at an exquisite turn-of-the-nineteenth-century church. Celebrated in French, it didn't matter that I couldn't understand, for we were all joined as one in this celebration. I just never realized how slight of stature the French-Canadian men and women were until today.

On returning, Parvin was ready to go for mid-morning brunch. I introduced her to a breakfast of French toast which we ate leisurely. She thoroughly enjoyed the new taste. We lingered over our coffee on the glass-enclosed porch overlooking the Richelieu River. I could see and feel her tranquility.

The warm day drew us to the large shady park on the grassy banks along the river. As we sat under a rustling tree, I was perfectly at ease with her in our solitude. I wandered in my mind back to the first day I met her those many months ago and how close I came to not knowing her, almost letting her slip away from me. Was it destiny? I believe so. She has taught me to learn about myself in so many ways, exploring my ability to express deep seated feelings in what some would say is poetry. And to think English class had never been my cup of tea.

"Hello Parvin! Come back!" With a giggle she said, "I let myself drift with the . . . what do you call them Fran?"

"Rapids."

"I let myself drift with the rapids and I was home for a little while, visiting the mountains near the Caspian Sea."

A park ranger approached and asked us to move to the sloping hill of the park. We noticed a group of men, numbering seventy to hundred, lining up in formation. They were dressed in eighteenth century French uniforms. They were getting ready to go on parade, carrying their colors and the French flag. Their military formations were crisp. It was quite a display. When it came to firing their muskets and cannons, Parvin became quite upset. "I do not like this." I wondered if she was thinking of her homeland under siege. Parvin had learned that the apartment she owned in Tehran had been damaged by a missile exploding in a nearby courtyard.

As the short weekend came to a close we wished we did not have to leave, and we knew there had been a drawing together of cultures, the blossoming of a unique friendship that would endure. Yes, it was meant to be.

Gifts

My lady, this is for you.
For gifts from the heart
More precious than the hand.

Your wisdom is a book of teaching
To quench a thirst for a world
So different than mine.
And I begin to understand.

Your joy radiates
Into trust and affection
Opening a heart to love.
And I found a special friend.

Your sensitivity is a portrait in kindness
To needs unspoken.
A melodious song without lyrics
And yet, I comprehend.

Your friendship of love
Is a soft light
That my eyes see and heart feels.
And my world is a better place.

Thank you my friend!

Wednesday, August 3

Margot wrote in the newsletter about the plans being formed for the reunion. Now she was asking former volunteers or others interested to call her if they planned on going or needed a ride. A bus would be rented by the Plattsburgh Kiwanis Club to provide transportation.

Ron Wood and Meredith O'Connor were occupied on this end lining up entertainment for the reunion, to be held on August 21st. Included were the talents of a professional clown Helen Berg, folksingers Cathy and Jerry Supple, and Ron planned to sing several selections as well.

I was busy keeping in contact with my group in Montréal trying to finalize a count as to how many to expect. I found on my follow-up calls that many Somalians and Sri Lankans would be working that day, but as far as I knew at this time, between two to three hundred could be expected. Robert and family, Oscar and family and Parvin did a super job with the difficult task of getting the information out. Without them there would have been no reunion.

Sunday, August 21

Today many would drive their own cars as we did. We took Rosemary, who had packed enough food for ten extra people, or so it seemed. We picked up Parvin, going on to Mont Royal where many had already arrived. Tables and chairs were dispersed under sunny blue skies but soon were placed in intimate groups of four or five.

The bus following Pat and Paul Cote's car from Plattsburgh finally arrived, carrying many former volunteers with Ron and Margot on board. Brian Smith, director of Crisis Center; Fran Wright, representing Social Services; Melinda Lee and Rolando, paralegals; Mrs. Allen, a language teacher to the many that were here; Mike Brassard, the former director of the National Guard shelter, were present. But it was Margot so many sought out, asking her to join in partaking from their international cuisine. And this special lady honored them by going from table to table, visiting and sampling tidbits to their

139

delight.

When I saw Robert, Sonia, and the girls, I could not believe my eyes, much less comprehend how they were able to carry so many dishes from their home on the South Shore while travelling by Metro, then bus, to Mont Royal. They proceeded to lay out on a long table a banquet of salads: Fapoush, Toboli, Failafel and Hommos, just to name a few dishes. They soon drew a crowd of fifteen or more. John and I were among the lucky ones who feasted on the delicious Lebanese food, and still there were leftovers.

The wonderful sunny day was spent eating and visiting with the many who had touched our lives. We relished the few success stories, such as Jimmie from Sri Lanka finding a job in his field of engineering. Tony from Suriname, South America, was a certified welder at the Montréal Ship Yard, and his wife, Linda, also worked. They had bought a home. Still others were seeking work, and job leads were exchanged among them. Their instilled pride and self-esteem dictated not to take from the government, but rather to make their own way.

The afternoon passed with great entertainment from Ron Wood and his group and the African Choir from Rev. Gibson's church. The gentle chants and songs were fascinating sounds to our ears.

At the end of the festivities, Margot, a very deserving lady, was pleasantly surprised to receive a memento from the Saint George Kiwanis Club of Montréal for her caring efforts. Then it was time to go.

Our day had been like a family reunion, with hugs and kisses, seeing so many for the first time in over a year. They remembered the staff and the volunteers from their first safe haven in the city of Plattsburgh. Truly it was an international reunion!

Reunion

They stopped as strangers
Not long ago,
The veil of mistrust dispersed
By kindness shown.

A reunion to celebrate
With friends from many nations
Begins in
The City of Lights.

Love blossomed
In Churchill Park
This August day,
Smiles warmer than sun-rays.

Music in the air
Even Santa was there,
Tables laden with food
Merrymaking in mid-afternoon.

Festivities end, goodbyes said,
Memories locked away
Of affections given
To Americans this special day.

Fall, 1988

Thursday, October 27

During the summer, Father Martin had said he would like to retire by fall. "I am only waiting for Bishop Brzana's approval."

Father would be sorely missed, for he had become such an integral part of the Refugee Relief Program over the past eighteen months. He always seemed to have room to take another young man under his wing, to be there to consult with when difficult problems arose.

I will always remember the day in 1987, just before Christmas, when I was asked by a Hindu couple if they might attend church. I explained it was a Mass said in Spanish. "It doesn't matter, it is a House of God. We will sit quietly in the back and pray." On arriving for Mass I asked, "Father, is it all right for them to attend?" "Fran, all are welcome."

After Mass, Father spoke with them and I saw his great compassion. He asked them to his home to share his Christmas dinner.

In October the Bishop granted Father Martin's retirement. After Father's last celebrated Mass a small farewell luncheon was held with joy and sorrow at Our Lady of Victory, with staff and volunteers in attendance.

Father Gerald Bolduc, OMI, prison chaplain at Dannemora, would replace him. Spanish Masses would continue, to the delight of everyone.

Monday, November 28

Our plans for Thanksgiving and Christmas turned out to be quite a task compared to last year, with so many refugees here.

The Salvation Army shared their table at Thanksgiving with some refugees, while local families invited others into their home. Still others cooked in their own apartments, making do with food from the Joint Council of Economic Opportunity.

Thursday, December 1

As the end of another year drew to a close I reflected over this very busy year.

With the weeks of the new year of 1988 giving way to months, positions of staff members changed. I was always amazed how flexible this program had become and how a need was somehow always answered.

Lynne Donaldson, who held Kathy Champagne's former job on a part-time basis for Social Services, took a full-time position with that agency. Maggie Talcott, who had been a volunteer translator and now was a part-time university student, stepped into Lynne's position. It would be a perfect job, for it would not interfere with Maggie's classes. Like Lynne, Maggie spoke French and Spanish, a helpful asset, since many displaced people either spoke one or the other.

As we approached spring it became evident there would be a housing shortage. Nellie Routt, owner of the Dawn Motel, had passed away in April, and the motel would close in early May. The Rip Van Winkle Motel, owned by Sue and Norman Landry, agreed to rent efficiency apartments until student housing became available for our use for the summer. Sundance Motel, owned by Winnie and Sandy Armstrong, had been renting to the refugees all along. However, the tourist season was about to start. This was the most profitable time for motels, which meant they would stop taking refugees. Getting the student housing as rentals for refugees was a great accomplishment by Lloyd.

The number of refugees appearing in Plattsburgh broke a record in June, with 116 seeking assistance. There was relief with the transition from using local motels to student housing.

The call for donations by Margot in the newsletters was increasing. It was answered one after another. The First Presbyterian Church adopted the paper "diapers project." They supplied disposable diapers to needy families upon hearing about the young couple who was diapering their baby in plastic bread wrappers. Saint Peter's Church started a collection of needed items and made weekly announcements of those needs. The United Methodist Women of Morrison-ville Church designated themselves as a collection point for donations. The Trinity Espiscopal Church continued their long-time support of Ann Allen's work as language teacher by purchasing dictionaries and reading material. There were donated services by a walk-in Health Care Center that did not charge sick refugees. Madan's Laboratory was doing free laboratory testing. The Salvation Army continued to take young men into their facilities in Syracuse.

The wish list in Margot's newsletter grew. Sheets, blankets, pillows, cots, towels, dishes, glasses, tableware, pots, pans, portable TVs, radios (days and nights were long for families), bicycles, toys, books, baby food and formulas were constantly in demand. Then the real crunch came, with university students returning at the end of August, student housing had to be vacated by mid-month.

Margot sought additional host homes, which would eventually evolve into a network from the northern regions of New York State into the state of Vermont. Lloyd found the Town and Beach Motel, six miles north of Plattsburgh on Route 9. Owner Sandra Conroy, agreed to rent to refugees for the winter. July saw 155 new arrivals with a record breaking 162 arriving in August. During this stressful period, 90 refugees returned to friends or relatives; 36 were in host homes, with 210 refugees living in our area.

There was another change of leadership when Pam Wilson replaced out-going regional director Denis Demers at Catholic Charities in September.

This was an excerpt from Margot's September *Refugee Relief Effort* newsletter:

> You have been so generous for so long . . . I thank you for this and hesitate to ask for more. But, the need is real. The wait is now seven months. A real strain on available resources. No longer can the supply of blankets, sheets, towels and dishes be

rotated. Our supply has been depleted. To bring the seriousness of this situation more sharply into focus, we now have families living in apartments with no beds, sharing a common blanket spread on the floor. Pots and pans are being shared between families. As donations arrive they are immediately distributed to those in need. The families staying in our area are committed to being as self-sufficient as possible, however these long stays are straining our resources. More host homes are needed.

In September, 156 more refugees came with hearings scheduled for May of 1989. Although October brought only 67 new arrivals, their hearing dates were also in May. In October there arrived hundreds of sheets, blankets and quilts from Jack Stantor of Day's Inn, a generous donation in answer to a desperate need.

Rita Jolicoeur, from the Retired Senior Volunteer Program, organized other volunteers, Margaret Erno and Delia Trombley, to manage the donations at Catholic Charities' garage; no small task with the abundance of winter outerwear arriving from the generous North Country people as we headed into fall. The Albany [NY] County Opportunity Inc. donated 200 women's and children's coats.

Friday, December 2

As Christmas approached Margot was looking for donated chickens or fresh vegetables to supplement the food baskets for the week before the holiday. Any monetary donations would go toward the purchase of something special, such as sugar or coffee. There would be practical gifts, "medical kits" made up of Band-aids, hand lotion, Chapstick, and cough syrup, organized and wrapped for gifts.

"If you would like to share a holiday meal, invite someone caroling or visit with a family, please call. I will match you with a teenager or a small or large family," Margot wrote in her December newsletter.

In November the John XXIII Newman Center at the State University at Plattsburgh and Psi Epsilon Chi Fraternity had collected food and money to make baskets for Catholic Charities to hand out to refugee families for Thanksgiving. The Newman Center, under Rev. Bill Muench, pastor, was going to supply chickens for every food box for Christmas.

The pleas for donations were being answered. Many paper bags, not only with items to make up the "medical kits," but also holding cookies and candy, mysteriously appeared on the back porch of Catholic Charities.

Individuals and organizations in Canada contacted Catholic Charities to lend support for the community's efforts in helping the refugees. Mabel Hastings and her youth group from the Eastern Township Citizens Advocacy in Montréal helped with gifts for the Christmas Party, to be held on a Saturday evening at Our Lady of Victory. They also planned to attend the Second Annual Christmas party.

Saturday, December 17

The young people from Montréal came bearing gifts of crayons, coloring books and puzzles for the children. The group spent hours fund-raising and presented a check to Margot for Catholic Charities to help with financial support for food, shelter and medical care. A dramatic show of support for the plight of the refugees.

It took volunteers two hours to get everyone to the party. Once again the large conference room and fireplace at OLV were adorned with holiday decorations. The room was packed; not an empty chair could be found! Off in one corner a glittering Christmas tree was surrounded with brightly wrapped gifts. The air buzzed with the excitement of those seeing their fellow countrymen. Refugees from Lebanon, Africa and Central America gathered together for a time to visit, a time to remember their faraway homelands. In one case it was a chance meeting, the discovery of a distant relative bringing hugs and tears.

I maneuvered my way through the crowd to Margot, asking, "Where did you find all these gifts for the refugees?"

"Many came from private donations received through the efforts of Meredith O'Connor. After the community needs were met, the extra gifts were donated through the Christmas Bureau and Catholic Charities," Margot replied with a cheerful smile. She was enjoying this gathering as much as anyone in this room and well she should, for all her work and effort radiated throughout the room. The holiday-decked tables were laden with enticing refreshments, all donated by volunteers. The feasting of over two hundred people soon mae it disappear!

HO, HO, HO! Saint Nick, Father Christmas, or Santa (Ron Wood) was back to the delight of everyone with his songs, storytelling and entertainment. Encircled by children with shining eyes, it took Santa over an hour to pass his gifts out to everyone this year. But he did not mind, for he too felt

Refugee Christmas party at Our Lady of Victory Secretarial School; Margot Zealis, Volunteer Coordinator. City of Plattsburgh. 1988.

the spirit of one in this international crowd. With a "Ho, Ho, Ho!" he departed for another year, to the disappointment of these children of the world.

As Santa left, a circle at one end of the room was formed by Eastern African men and women. A soft chant became louder in rhythm with their clapping hands. Two women, each wearing a long colorful "dirac" (dress) stepped into the circle and began to dance. With arms held above their heads, they too kept a clapping beat as they wove artfully in and around within the circle, drawing an international audience. We had been fascinated by the joyous unfamiliar "Amin Alahoyow," a traditional song of worship sung earlier, and now by their dance. You could feel the merriment building as the beat resounded throughout. Unexpectedly, the two women broke the circle and took Margot by the hand, drawing her back in with them. There was a roar of approval as Margot attempted their native steps, proving to be quite good.

Then the most heart rending song began. Those present did not have to understand Arabic to know Imad was singing of his homeland, Lebanon. With tears flowing from fellow countrymen, we all stood in silence, listening to words understood only by our hearts.

Imad had been depressed since arriving alone in October, having left his wife and three children in war-torn Lebanon. However, tonight he was feeling jubilation, "There is so much beauty. Love should be the law of the world."

Truly, brotherhood and sisterhood was seen this evening. Drawn together by songs and dance, they did not want this time to end.

Harmony

It is the season of hope,
To celebrate in dance,
A circle of jubilation

And clapping of hands.

A time of remembrance
Of loved ones far away.
Songs sung with passion
Of homeland under seige.

No barrier of language
For hearts understand
The meaning of love
And "good will to man."

Time stands still
In a magical way,
For we are not strangers
This special day.

So join in the song of harmony,
See the joy of peace,
Feel the love intoxicate a tiny room
As people of the world
Come together as one.

Monday, December 19

With the year nearing its end, John and I left to join our
friends in Montréal to celebrate Christmas the Sunday before
the twenty-fifth. The weather was kind, a beautiful, not-too-
cold day. This year we would have a new stop to visit Robert
and Sonia before going on to Oscar's family, where Parvin
would join us.

We had made many trips to Robert and his family since
their reunion in March. Their warm hospitality to John and
me made us feel right at home. Today we would have Lebanese pastries and coffee at Sonia's home, with an evening
meal at Oscar's. How lucky can we be to have two international treats in one day! I was sure John and I would not be
eating for the next few days.

"Merry Christmas," greeted us as we were welcomed
with warm hugs and kisses into this large airy apartment,

graced with holiday decorations.

The pastry was delicious. Robert is a master chef in Montréal, but Sonia's forte is her pastries and cakes. Merei and Alice kept our coffee cups filled and saw to it that our plates were never completely empty. We finally pleaded, "Please, no more." The hours passed all too quickly in the company of this dear family. All too soon it was time to bid farewell, knowing that Merei and Alice were doing well at work in the specialty shop in downtown Montréal. Alice would enroll next year in high school to complete her studies. Sonia, who prepared evening meals several times a week for private families, and Robert, who worked six days a week, were determined one day to own their own bakery or restaurant. And as we drove toward Oscar's I thought about the past year that had brought so many changes.

Maritza and Percy were now living in Toronto where Maritza was working as a secretary at an insurance company. Percy was working for United Parcel Service. Their decision to leave Montréal and move to Toronto was the right choice, but John and I certainly missed our visits with them. Still, after two years for Percy, they have not received permanent status, which means they cannot send for Laura. And their pain continues.

Jamie, dear Jamie, I had worried needlessly about her, for she was doing just great in Montréal. I had visited her several times when I knew she would be free from working the two jobs she was holding. On one job she worked nights at her uncle's restaurant, and the other as an interpreter during the day at a law firm that specialized in refugee problems. This last job led to a full time position as a receptionist/secretary. However, she also enrolled in night classes, taking Spanish to further her education which might lead to a higher position. Her father, Marcel, arrived in the spring with a three-week stay in Plattsburgh. He was a kind gentleman who had seen his war-torn country slowly die. Jamie's mother and two sisters flew directly into Montréal in late summer and were allowed to stay. Finally they were together once again as a family.

I will not soon forget the call in March from a distraught Cora asking me to come to speak with Maria. Maria wanted to return to her country. That weekend, John and I made an unscheduled trip to Montréal.

As I listened to Maria, she had many good reasons to go home. She said, "The call I received from my country is not the reason why I want to go." She found life in Montréal too difficult. She could no longer cope with the demeaning status of refugee. Maria had sought to continue her college studies but the cost made it impossible. Again, because of her status she would pay the same as any other foreign student. She saw no future for herself in Canada. Being nineteen made her very impatient; life was passing her by. She said the young man's call was not a reason for her to return; only that she wanted to continue her studies. I felt differently. However, she was of age to make her own decisions. I did not try to talk her out of it. Cora was devastated when Maria left at the end of May. Cora was under great stress, for she knew also that her mother was very ill in El Salvador. Maria was home less than a month when her grandmother passed away. It helped Cora to know Maria was there. Maria took on the responsibilities of her mother, fulfilling the duties of a loving daughter who could not be there.

Maria did enroll in college and in the fall she married the young man who had made the call. Both are continuing their college studies.

Oscar had not received any responses to his resumes, nor did the door open to him upon his completing and passing his real estate exam. On receiving his license, he approached several real estate agencies. However, once they knew his status as a refugee the doors closed. They would not give him an opportunity to prove himself until Canada accepted him as a permanent resident. By meeting Leroy, Rev. Gibson's right hand man, (while planning the summer reunion), Oscar had made a contact. As a result, Oscar was hired as a business manager for a private company that grew natural herbs and grains. It was a start. Cora was a baby sitter, becoming quite attached to a little boy. She was not totally happy. She wanted a better job where she could be with people. As a former teacher she missed and needed human contact.

Sandra and Erika were excelling in school and had many friends. "Montréal is where I want to stay. I do not want to return to my country to live," Erika told me on one of our visits.

Parvin had finished her French course. She was about to enter a four-month program where the students in the last month would have to find, on their own, five different businesses each week, go to them, seek employment, and fill out a form provided by the program on each place they went. She was hopeful, looking forward to the program starting.

We finally arrived at Oscar's. "Merry Christmas" resounded as John and I stepped into welcoming arms. One after another, Oscar, Cora, Sandra, Erika and then Parvin. The new apartment was ablaze in holiday decorations. It was alive with the spirit of the season. What a difference from last year! With the wonderful aromas filling the air, I would be justified in satiating my appetite.

Another year had passed in the lives of our dear friends, a year filled with hope and disappointments, sadness and joy. But today we took pleasure and counted our blessings that we were together once again for this holiday season.

Winter, 1988

Friday, December 23

"Every time I think I've heard the most shocking story, I hear something else that tops it," Darlene, the health nurse, said.

A twelve-year-old girl arrived with her mother from El Salvador just before Christmas. They were placed in a host home, where the host family realized something was wrong with the little girl. Upon questioning by Darlene, she knew the little girl must be seen by a gynecologist. The diagnosis was not good. She would need surgery as soon as possible. When the little girl was six years old she had been run over by a truck which ruptured her lower abdominal cavity. Perhaps it was because of the lack of medical knowledge or equipment that her body organs had not been placed back in the proper positions. Some were even missing. Darlene turned to Brian Smith, who immediately contacted authorities in Montréal. The slow wheels of justice turned quickly with this emergency. A Prime Minister's Permit was issued directly from the Canadian government, thus allowing mother and daughter entry within seventy-two hours of their arrival in Plattsburgh. It was a great Christmas gift for mother and daughter. This was the first of three Prime Minister Permits that would be received from the Canadian government for refugee medical reasons.

Monday, December 26

During this period of time between our two holidays refugees were still arriving, although the numbers were much lower. Many were applying and gaining direct entry into Canada. However, some cases caused great stress. Such was the case for two families. The men had applied at a different time and were accepted into Canada while their wives and children were left here until April, a terribly long separation with only telephone calls relieving their loneliness. The strength of these wives and mothers did not break under the long days and longer nights. Many tears were shed due to not understanding Canada's policy that would keep families apart.

Saturday, December 31

The end of 1988 would show 1400 refugees had passed through this year with many still in Plattsburgh. One hundred fifty households had been set up. Over 400 blankets and 900 sheets had gone out to refugees. Approximately 400 refugees had been helped by host homes. Hundreds of people had been outfitted through donations at Catholic Charities and the Salvation Army Store on Montcalm Street, the latter staffed with kindness by Elsie Ciccone, Jerry Breyette and George Donah. Thousands of hours were given by volunteers.

"A burden shouldered in a quiet and humble manner," as Margot put it.

Friday, January 6

Paul, Pat, Sue and I found on the days we worked that the van was full with supplemental food boxes when we left our pick-up point at the Joint Council of Economic Opportunity to deliver throughout the city. There was no shortage of willing hands to help with the current six to seven month wait which the refugees found almost intolerable. They were hostages to time and willing to help in any way.

Jose, from El Salvador, walked from the First Presbyterian Church, located downtown where he and his family were being hosted, to Catholic Charities a mile away, seeking to assist in some way. Steve Patnode obliged by giving him a shovel to clear the snow from the sidewalk and driveway that had fallen overnight. I had just returned from doing an errand when I saw Jose standing in puzzlement. "Hi Jose, going to clear the sidewalk?"

"Yes, but where do I put the snow?" A reasonable question from one who had never seen snow before.

As drivers we were not only the eyes and ears for the program but came to intimately know many of the families. Often we were invited in for a cup of coffee, breaking up their boring day. If time allowed we would enjoy the strong Turkish coffee that satisfied us for the rest of the day. So it was with John from Lebanon.

Each day John would help the volunteers with deliveries. He would often show me where new families lived or if they had been missed in receiving a food box. I would make a note for a box for the following day. I came to believe he knew Plattsburgh and the food program better than me.

The Cotes had become quite close to this family, and with the six month waiting period coming to a close, John, with his wife Noha, and daughters, Narimane and Darine, wanted to do something special. Not only for the Cotes, but for staff and volunteers. Noha cooked for three days in her small efficiency apartment at the Sundance. How this was possible I'll never understand. Margot, Darlene, Paul and Pat, Lloyd and his wife Karen, Winnie, who owned Sundance, my husband John and I were all guests at a traditional Lebanese feast that lasted well into late evening. It was their way of saying "thank you" and an end to a very long stay.

I never suspected I would come face to face with a fundamentalist "Islamic belief" with the next pair of willing hands, a belief that would encircle the world.

Wednesday, January 11

"Have you read the book?" Oh, oh, here it comes! I had been forewarned by Margot this morning as to Hussan's feelings about author Salman Rushdie and his book "The

Satanic Verses." It was making world headlines!

A rather concerned Margot had told me, "He helped Sue on Friday and it will be the last time. She will not take him with her anymore. He told Sue it would be an honor for him to kill Rushdie if he could. I just want you to be aware, Fran."

Volunteers and staff had a policy of not discussing race, politics or religion. We were here only to help in humanitarian ways. Not to say I had not spoken of religion or politics with friends I had made, for I had, but in a proper setting. Well, this was going to be interesting.

"No, Hussan, I haven't."

"Why not?"

"I am not familiar with your religion and if I read the book I would not understand," I replied.

"You know, Khomenei is right. He should be taught a lesson."

"Hussan, to kill someone is a pretty permanent lesson. You are in the West now. People have the right to say and to write what they wish. You may not agree, but this is what is so wonderful about living in a democracy. The right to speak your mind without fear." Our discussion continued in a friendly and quite frank way. By the time we arrived at the Sundance he said, "Perhaps you are right. I feel I understand better. Please, come have coffee with Maggie and me."

I liked Hussan, this neatly dressed, educated engineer from Lebanon. He was quite informed on Western ways, and a caring person; when Paul Cote was ill in the hospital Hussan asked me if I would take him to visit Paul. He had helped me make deliveries over the past weeks and made the mornings pass quickly talking about his country. Hussan had told me in passing that his wife was Christian and he was Moslem. It did not matter to them, for there was only one God. I had made

156

no comment on hearing this. I just listened to the difficulties they had faced from this mixed religious marriage in their country, not being accepted by his family and Maggie's family. Maggie had been a volunteer at the Red Cresent organization in Lebanon. Religion did not matter; she just enjoyed helping people. To help pass the time he cooked, giving me goodies to bring home, taking delight when I told him how delicious they were.

Did I make a small difference in Hussan's perception? I hope so, for I truly liked him.

Thursday, January 19

A new law was ushered in with the new year of 1989 affecting applicants seeking refugee status in Canada. People now applying at the border would go through a three-step process:

1. Interview: At this time they must request refugee status and are briefly interviewed as to their intent.
2. Inquiry: Is scheduled within one to five days. This phase addresses the admissibility, eligibility and credibility of the claimant. From here the individual is either refused entry or scheduled for the final hearing.
3. Hearing: They can now be refused refugee status or granted final acceptance.

Only time only would tell how well the new law would work. If waiting times for hearings once again increased, would the new system become overloaded with people being returned to Plattsburgh? In any case, the agencies involved in assisting the refugee population were still dedicated to meeting the need for food and shelter.

Many were struggling to support themselves as each month went by. It is expensive for anyone to live six or seven months in a community without employment. Under the law, refugees awaiting entry into Canada could not be employed.

This was the case of one family with a hearing date in April. They were discreetly selling their jewelry to pay for their apartment and to buy food to supplement what was given them. They had not complained and were upset when Crisis Center found out. Margot found a host home for them.

Then there was the man from Québec who came to Plattsburgh, approached a Somalian woman traveling alone with her children and offered to buy her baby. This was only revealed when the mother, who spoke French, told Celine Mac Dougall, one of the translators. The city police were waiting when he returned to once again offer money to the mother. District Attorney Penelope D. Clute charged him with harassment. He posted a $100 bail and returned to Québec. He was to re-appear in court at a later date, but never did. However, the Royal Canadian Mounted Police became interested and came to interview the refugee woman involved.

I do not know if Canadian authorities pursued this matter further, but I wondered what rock this low-life crawled out from under!

It was not long into the New Year when the waiting period inched up to three weeks. We were fortunate that in the first month of the year the number of people seeking help was only fifty-one.

In January there was another change of position. Maggie Talcott decided to enroll as a full-time student to complete her degree. It had been difficult for her to balance her time between family, college and internship with the Crisis Center. Maggie had been involved with the Refugee Relief Program from the very beginning, volunteering when and wherever she was needed. Staff and volunteers would dearly miss her.

Karen Loehide, who would replace Maggie until May, planned special trips for the refugee children in our area. The children found the days long with nothing to look forward to. Many children of families, who had six to seven month waits under the old law, had enrolled in local public and private schools. The children of families under the new law with stays of four weeks had too short a time to justify enrolling them in school. Karen took the children to Pizza Hut, and on another outing to the city fire station. They were pleasure trips creating special memories for these children.

Tuesday, March 7

We had been very fortunate over the years, with the thousands that spent weeks and months here, that we had not experienced any tragedies, but we nearly had one. A young man from El Salvador fell from a third floor apartment window where he had been renting an apartment with several other young men. Striking his head on the pavement had left him in a coma. The doctors at the Medical Center in Plattsburgh operated. They did not know if he would survive, or if he did, what his condition would be.

After many weeks he began to respond to outside stimulus. Hospital officials asked for aid in his recovery by daily visits from those who spoke Spanish. Ismial did not speak or understand English. The response was overwhelming! Rolando went often; Father Bolduc went just about every day. Someone brought a cassette player with Spanish tapes and nurses would continually play them. Someone else paid the rental for a TV set to provide additional stimulus.

The time came for physical therapy. His muscles were atrophying. There was a catch, however. The hospital needed a signed consent to start the therapy. Rolando came forward and offered to try to get in touch with his family in El Salvador. This was a tremendous undertaking considering Ismial came from a small village in the countryside that had no running water and no electricity, much less telephones.

Rolando did accomplish what he had set out to do. A letter of consent was received by the CVPH Medical Center and Ismial began receiving physical therapy.

After four months Ismail opened his eyes and would stare at the visual stimulus without acknowledging the presence of anyone that might be in the room. I went with Margot to see Ismial after we had gone to visit Paul Cote, who was also in the hospital at that time. He gave no response to our presence. However, there was progress. By early summer he was talking and had regained some use of his hands and legs. Truly it was a miracle, but he had a long way to go.

Spring, 1989

Tuesday, March 28

As told to me by a dear friend, during "Holy Week" in El Salvador Catholics celebrate Easter in a traditional way. The celebration starts on Palm Sunday with a procession. They seek to relive each day of the first Holy Week until Easter Sunday, a reenactment of what happened two thousand years ago.

The people who participate in this procession sometimes have to wait two years before they can take part. It is very popular and a great honor to take part in this celebration. They will even pay in order to be in it, and provide their own long purple gowns with a cone-shaped purple headdress which completely covers the head except for the holes cut out for the eyes.

On Holy Thursday there is a silent procession for men only. The procession starts at eight o'clock at night with each man carrying a lighted candle. They sing and pray for repentance until midnight.

On Holy Friday (Good Friday), the procession starts early

in the morning. The highlight is the huge procession with forty men carrying a platform on which is the fallen Jesus holding his cross. They stop at stations along the way to pray and meditate. They finish by 3:00 in the afternoon.

On Holy Saturday the glorious mothers spank (lightly) their small children so they will grow tall, according to legend.

On Easter Sunday there is a large festival, the biggest of all. On a flat-bed truck there is a float representing the world with a risen Jesus high above it. Joyful music fills the air as people parade down the street, with hundreds lining the processional route.

Easter was approaching. In the newsletter, Margot made an appeal for fresh vegtables or fruit. The donations would be added to the food baskets made up of canned goods that went out each week, helping to feed the 130 people in our area. The local people responded with donations, and others called Margot to tell her they would take Christian refugee families to church on this traditional Holy Day.

Monday, April 17

Two letters arrived, one from a Sri Lankan family who had been in our area for four months and one from a Somalian family who had been hosted by an area family for over six months. I think they say it all:

> I want to thank you from the bottom of our hearts for all your pains and interest taken to look after the refugees like us in Plattsburgh.

The second letter, from the Somalian family, went to the Editor at the *Press-Republican*. Margot received a copy as well.

> As our family prepares to enter Canada as refugees in early May, we would like to express our deep appreciation to all in

Plattsburgh area who have been kind and generous to us and others like us while we pass through the United States in our flight from military and political violence on our way to safety in Canada.

You have been our friends among strangers; you have clothed, sheltered, and fed us while we have been unable to provide these things for ourselves. You have personally demonstrated the human kindness of the American people which contrasts with governmental acts of power and majesty.

While violations of basic human rights continue to keep this fragile world in turmoil, we hope that you will find it in your hearts to continue the work of caring for other refugees as you have cared for us. Together we struggle for a world at peace.

We hope that you will never suffer the loss of homeland and family, the loss of human dignity and rights, the loss of civil rights and protection. We hope that you and your children will enjoy and prosper with all people of the earth. Once again, we recognize your generous hospitality, and we look forward to the pleasure of your calls and visits when we become settled in Canada. We shall never forget you.

Abdullah and family
Potsdam, NY

The loving support given by the North Country people!

Monday, May 1

Many of us believed the Philippines to be a staunch ally of our country. Yet, political persecutions did take place. Such was the case of Lydia.

Lydia was a math teacher in the Phillippines, which leads one to believe she would not be seen as a threat to that country. This was true to a point. However, because of the position she held and her personal beliefs in justice, a leftist group threatened her and her family. Lydia had to flee the country with her teenage son and three young daughters. Her husband, who was a merchant seaman, was at sea. Perhaps he, too, would have been persecuted or threatened, just for being her spouse

162

and not for his beliefs.

Lydia and her children spent five weeks in Plattsburgh before her entry date into Canada. During that time she was an elementary teacher's aid at Saint Peter's Catholic School, where her daughters were enrolled and other refugee children had, or were, studying.

Lydia's son, who had entered into veterinary studies in the Philippines, went each day to Champlain Valley Veterinary Services to give his time wherever needed. He thoroughly enjoyed each and every hour he spent there. Lydia and her son certainly were not "takers" but "givers."

Lydia was also very active within the First Presbyterian Church while she was here. She asked for, and was warmly given, approval to prepare a Philippine dinner to be given in "thanksgiving," using the church's kitchen facilities. It would be served to her guests the night before she and her family were to enter Canada. Her brother, who lived in Ontario, brought all the necessary food and ingredients to prepare the meal.

Margot, Darlene, Rolando, John and I were invited to attend. In attendance were Presbyterian pastor Dr. Earl S. Johnson, Jr., and associate pastor Rev. Thomas McKinnon, along with many parishioners. Sisters from several Catholic orders were invited and attended.

As we arrived, Lydia gave each and every one a small candle which mystified me and, I am sure, everyone else. She asked us to gather together and light the candles. When all candles were lit the lights were turned off. Standing in front of the gathering with her own lit candle she began to speak, using the symbolically lit candle in a spiritual way. This is the gist of a portion of her humble words:

> Alone in darkness my family and I came. This small candle that I hold by itself is a small light in my world of darkness.

Together, you have lit my world of darkness with bright light. My family and I are no longer alone. We thank you and we shall never forget.

We were all touched to the core of our being.

In an interview, Dominican Sister Debbie Blow, principal of Saint Peter's, said her "international friends" were not "takers." When offered items for play, such as art supplies, the children politely declined. Instead they chose necessities for survival, like clothing or a book to learn the language.

Sister Debbie believed that their fresh perspective on daily taken-for-granted habits and possessions had given Saint Peter's students a healthy vision.

The Saint Peter's principal also believed that her students would receive other benefits from their companionship with students from El Salvador, Hungary, Somalia and Ethiopia. She hoped that they would learn that "we are all equal in the eyes of the Lord." It's not "us" and "them" but rather "we."

Saturday, May 27

I received wonderful news with a call from Parvin in early spring. She had received her Landed Immigrant papers. She had been accepted by Canada!

Parvin's roommate Sussan had gone back to Iran earlier this year, and Parvin had moved once again into another apartment, with Aram as her roommate. After successful heart surgery, Aram was back at McGill University working toward her Masters Degree in political science.

In late spring Parvin was in the latter part of her program, and was out each day visiting businesses. On her own, she went to an Anglophone High School and was referred to the Protestant School Board of Greater Montréal, where she met Ann Peacock, who was an administrator there. Parvin was hired to assist in correcting high school student papers. She had to learn the operation of a computer, which she did, feeling somewhat back in her academic element. She was happy.

However, I felt deep in the recesses of my mind that she would be leaving Montréal. I held this belief because of both what she said, and did not say. I did not ask her outright, for I did not want to know. I was not prepared for the loss of not seeing my friend nor the pain it would bring.

Summer, 1989

Friday, June 30

Known to many refugees as "father," Lloyd Mori would be leaving his position as Crisis Center Refugee Program Coordinator to accept a position in the private sector. Lloyd had been an integral part of this program since the 1987 shelter period, where he had been a staff member.

I would miss Lloyd. There had been times over the years when I had turned to him out of frustration and he would make a comment that turned my near tears into laughter. I will always remember our steaming cups of coffee warming us as we stood in the early morning chill outside the shelter. It now seems so long ago, our quiet and not so quiet talks. It will always be his spontaneous laughter I will miss the most. Now to whom would I "pass the buck!"

The answer would be Kim Couryer from Social Services, who would fill in for one month. Gretchen Alsip would then take the position until the end of August, when she would be moving south. I now thoroughly understood the phrase, "The more things change, the more they stay the same."

Once again the refugees were being housed in vacant student housing for the summer. However, those arriving in late spring had an increase in their waiting for their hearing entry dates of up to six weeks.

A sudden influx of 77 refugees at the beginning of summer caught the Relief Program off guard, especially one weekend with the arrival of 31. The flow of refugees had slowed since the new immigration laws went into effect in Canada at the beginning of the year. The refugee staff at Crisis Center had been cut back when Karen Loehide, who represented Social Services, left in May. She was not replaced. It all fell on Gretchen's shoulders. She had only been on the job two and a half weeks when the group of 31 arrived. Usually one or two refugees had been coming each day, taking about two days to process each one. On this particular weekend, Gretchen woke up to discover 26 had arrived and then received a call that five more were on the way. The little room at Crisis Center was overflowing with luggage, adults and crying children.

Public Health Nurse Darlene Edwards obtaining medical information from young men from El Salvador at clinic at Presbyterian Church. 1989.

When a reporter asked if there was some reason they all came at the same time, she answered, "That was low on our priority list of things to ask them."

Darlene was working hard to health screen all the new arrivals from Somalia, Central America and Lebanon. She found the primary health problems of people were due to traveling long distances, under extreme stress. Eating irregularly during their travel and now finding themselves in a strange climate, they were surrounded by an alien culture with a language they could not speak. Darlene knew from past experiences she would find them more relaxed and secure after they had rested.

> We had enough sheets, blankets and dishes to help each family. It is a constant source of amazement to me and others who watch our work that you continue to respond to the ongoing needs of the Refugee Relief Effort. Thank you for answering our prayers and those of the 3,500 refugees who have sought assistance during their lonely and frightening journey to freedom.

This was an excerpt from Margot's July 1989 *Refugee Relief Effort* newsletter, which included the number of refugees helped since the program began in late 1986. Student housing had become full and many of the refugees in our area had been taken in by host homes.

Monday, July 3

The refugees living in apartments were now receiving food vouchers instead of food boxes from JCEO to supplement their dietary needs. Each voucher had a limited amount of money that depended upon the size of the family. The food vouchers were available through a grant that Margot had worked very hard for and received.

The drivers would take the refugees to the Grand Union where they could choose their food of fresh meat, fresh fruit, fresh vegtables, etc., but not alcoholic beverages or cigarettes. At times they would overspend the amount of their voucher by a few cents and did not have the money to pay. I saw on many occasions a particular cashier at a local supermarket, named Frances, take from her own purse and pay the difference. A very special lady who always spoke kindly to them. I have seen her reach out and touch their hand or lean across the counter and give them a hug saying, "May God watch over you."

A new lunch program consisting of a cup of soup, beverage and sandwich was arranged with Najya's, a local diner named after its owner, on Clinton Street, while Our Lady of Victory Secretarial School was closed for the summer. The new arrivals would go there for lunch while being processed at the Crisis Center. This food program was supported through the donations of individuals and churches, both locally and nationally.

The "jelly shelf," as it was affectionately called, was supplied with crackers, peanut butter, jelly, jars of applesauce and other non-cooking foods. The items were donated to Catholic Charities for Margot to distribute to refugees until they had been processed and could move into apartments with a kitchen. The procedure usually took one or two days. All food was donated by the caring hearts of North Country people!

Saturday, August 5

What I did not want to know or hear came to pass. Parvin would be leaving Montréal to return to her native land.

It was only last month that Rosemary, dear Rosemary, had left with her boys, Ben and Colin, to join her husband Bob in Spain. They would be stationed there for the next three years. I missed our twice-weekly meetings for coffee, our semi-monthly trips to Montreal, our "other world," just the two of us, with her fast asleep beside me on our return in the wee hours. I missed one friend already, and now the unthinkable was going to happen.

"It is something I must do, Fran, not only for my uncle and family, but for myself. There are so many things I have to attend to. My mother's things, the repairing of my apartment. My uncle can no longer watch over my empty home. You know my uncle is like a father to me. I must go back to see him. He is not well, he is getting up in years. I hope when I return I will be freer in my mind."

I sat with a heart as heavy as stone, listening to what I had hoped I would never hear. "When do you leave? When will you return?," I asked with so many thoughts flashing through my mind.

"I will leave within two months, and hope to return in six months," was her painful reply. "Oh Fran, I am being pulled. I am being torn between two worlds."

And I felt guilty for wanting her to stay. What right did I have? Granted, our relationship had grown into a unique friendship, but her uncle was her family, I was only a friend. I felt I was being selfish. Why did I feel so strongly about her going? Was it because I feared for her safety? Yes. Was it because I felt once she returned she would stay? Yes, I did. Why would she want to come back if, as she said, it was safe for her to return to her country? Home is where the heart is, and hers was in her native land. Perhaps deep within, this was my greatest fear, that I would never see her again.

The amount of time before she left would now be short. Plans were made for a last short weekend to spend together.

I scoured a Québec map searching for a locality not too far from Montréal. A special place where quality time could be spent with a friend whom I had come to love like a sister. A niche for happy memories, not sad, that would bridge our separation.

Sunday, August 13

It was a beautiful day in late summer when I headed north. I stopped first at the Québec Information Center, to ask about the village of Saint Agathe nestled in the Laurentians. I would not be disappointed with my choice from all the account given by the helpful, courteous young lady.

Neither Parvin nor I had ever been in the heart of the Laurentians, which was only 45 minutes from the city. It was not long via the auto-route before we turned onto a secondary road into the heart of the mountains. On rounding a curve, there before us was Lac des Sables (Lake of Sands), rimmed by the small village of Saint Agathe.

We took the last available room (a suite), in a new three-story motel with balconies which had been recommended. It snuggled among trees on the side of a hill, overlooking a picturesque setting of the village and an emerald lake surrounded by mountains.

The rest of the morning was spent exploring the quaint shops and having a leisurely late lunch at an outdoor cafe. We returned to enjoy afternoon coffee on the motel's terrace, amid the aura of all this beauty. The streets were alive with strolling people as we went for our evening meal in a charming little restaurant adorned with hanging plants. Parvin did not miss any chance to record our experiences in photographs.

The next morning, leaving Parvin sleeping, I went down for coffee before going on to Mass and found the owner setting up for breakfast. I learned that she knew where Plattsburgh was, that she and her husband came often to shop and enjoy our beaches. Small world.

I left for church but, finding I was early, I drove toward the lake to explore more. I came upon a park with beds and beds of blooming flowers. Well, this would take up the day, for I planned to return with Parvin.

Upon my return, I found Parvin out on the balcony taking pictures again! We went down to a continental breakfast of fresh fruit, fresh baked French bread, cheese, meats, juice and coffee. Then it was time to check out.

We drove to the park, which Parvin loved, taking more photos. Is there no end? Buses arrived with people who would take an afternoon excursion on the lake. We were content to just talk, building happy memories in the liveliness and beauty of this special place. We lingered over lunch in the park restaurant, putting off our departure from this fabulous weekend.

Today

Journey with me to a land of enchantment.
See the emerald amid a mountain necklace of green,
Where farewell is only a fantasy of the mind
And tomorrow is an eternity away.

Enter a haven nestled in silent woods.
Come gently lest this fragile heart shatters,
Letting my salty tears mingle
With the bittersweet wine of happiness.

Gaze with me on quiet waters
As cherished words become a string of pearls.
A treasured keepsake to be worn;
To remember is to be alive.

Stroll with me along a path of efflorescent flowers.
Savor the joyous laughter,
Sing once more your haunting songs.
These golden hours will always be my rosemary.

Share with me one last time
A banquet for body and soul,
Lift the wine glass in salute
Of two spirits united by love.

Speak not of farewell or oceans apart,
For my full heart selfishly holds
These precious moments in solitude,
For today is all of my tomorrows.

Thursday, August 31

Once again in mid-August, with the returning of students at the end of the month, refugee housing was found at local motels or in host homes.

With Greyhound Bus Lines facing $10,000 fines, efforts were made on their part to prevent these travelers from buying tickets from any point in the United States to Montréal without papers. However, it did not produce a slow-down.

A refugee without the proper papers or visa would be taken off the bus in Plattsburgh. They would then hire a cab to take them to the Canadian border to claim Refugee Status. The driver of the cab would let them off a half-mile before the border where they would walk the rest of the way, whether it was winter or summer. Nor did it matter if they were single or a family. Otherwise, the cab driver or anyone else would be charged by Canadian authorities with transporting illegals. Those who could not afford a cab often walked from Plattsburgh to the border and back; a distance of 20 miles one way. I knew of several cases where men had done this. Until these people had the proper papers they could not be brought into the Refugee Relief Program.

The time came to bid farewell to Gretchen Alsip, the Crisis Center Refugee Program Coordinator for the past three months. She would be moving to Atlanta, Georgia. Gretchen had done a super job under very trying circumstances.

Diane Rolfs was her replacement, bringing with her many talents. She was fluent in Spanish, as she had lived in Central and South America for 16 years as the daughter of a diplomat. She understood and had real compassion for the plight of the refugees.

Diane had come to the North Country when Bob, her husband, accepted a position in the medical community. "If I had one place to call home, it would be Montana," was her reply when I asked where her roots were.

She enrolled at Plattsburgh State University to continue working toward her Master's Degree in counseling by taking night courses. I wondered how this lovely young lady would be able to cope with the demands of being a wife, mother, student and the stress that this job brings.

Her first week in the position saw two large families arrive within a few days of each other, a family of 14 and a family of 9. The number of refugees seeking aid was increasing steadily, and for the first time in several months the number of refugees in the area went over 120.

Monday, September 4

Our Lady of Victory Secretarial School reopened for the fall semester, and with it the refugee hot lunch program was reinstated. New arrivals would be taken to the secretarial school cafeteria for lunch, as in the past, to enjoy once again the great meals prepared by Bev Frasier.

The following paragraph is an excerpt from one of Margot's newsletters.

> The lunch program was "kicked off" with a donation from a couple in Hammond, New York who on their second honeymoon decided to help others in "thanks" for the wonderful years they have had together. They arrived at Catholic Charities with a truck filled with donations they had collected from friends and neighbors in their area. Their concern about the food needs of the refugees came from their past donations to the shelter. When they learned that the refugees were no longer eating in a communal situation, they donated funds to support this fall's hot lunch program at Our Lady of Victory. Thank

you for thinking of others during your celebration, Alma and Howard! HAPPY ANNIVERSARY!

Sunday, September 10

I did not know that Parvin had applied for and received a visitor's visa from the American Embassy in Montréal to come to our home for a long weekend, her first visit since she went to Canada.

My best friend Mary Jane Moschelle and I took Parvin for a day's outing, first to the top of Whiteface Mountain and then on to Lake Placid.

While Parvin was here she finished a colored pencil drawing of a young lady wearing a bonnet and attired in a long colorful gown. She stood in a doorway with her hand on an open door with a flower garden in the background. It said it all, "Welcome." Parvin gave it as a gift to John and me.

Chris, Mike and the children came to spend a few days, enjoying her Iranian meals of many dishes, and to say good-by.

I took Parvin back to Montréal. I was greatly surprised when Akbar called a few days later to say they would be coming down. Apparently Parvin so enjoyed her visit that Akbar wanted to come before she left. John and I were delighted!

This time John gave us a tour of his territory of out-of-the-way places, a covered bridge, river rapids, unknown spectacular views of Whiteface Mountain, and on to Lake Placid. We strolled the narrow streets and little shops. Akbar loved it. He is a man in tune with nature.

Fall, 1989

Then came what I had not looked forward to, the day I went to Montréal to say good-bye. I tried not to look beyond the daylight hours, but instead enjoyed these fleeting moments visiting with Parvin and friends. I did not want to face that final moment, not knowing what to say, but it came. With a facade of encouraging words our emotions were held within, but under the illuminating street-light true feelings were made visible.

As I pulled away in the car, she walked toward the entrance with a final wave. I knew in my heart our friendship would be steadfast. Would I ever see her again? I truly did not believe so.

It was a long, lonely drive home.

Pajvak
(Echo)

Let the river of tears carry
The bittersweet memories back to me
As I sit beside the swift rapids
That sweep your voice away.

Where once we sat beside the still waters
And spoke of dreams of what could be
A prevailing wind now surrounds me
And I hear your haunting songs in the pajvak of rustling leaves.

I travel in the valley of solitude
Amid mountains silhouetted by a fiery sunset,
I turn towards the warmth of your laughter
And there is only silence.

Wings of darkness cover my heart
Where once a light burned brightly.
A saddened spirit searches for your image

In the empty blackness of my starless universe.

Wistfully I walk alone in the shadow of memories
Listening for the voice that fills me
With the pajvak of love,
"I will come back, I will return."

Wednesday, October 4

Although the food program was being taxed to the limits in early fall, a hot meal was still provided to newcomers. The program also continued helping those in need with food vouchers.

Margot applied and received approval for the refugee food program to qualify as a Food Pantry. Therefore she was able to order specific food items, such as rice and a variety of dry beans, at an inexpensive price from the Albany Food Bank in the state capital. They were food items that she knew were diet staples in the many cultures of the arriving refugees.

When Margot asked if I knew where she might get a freezer or a refrigerator, I told her I would check with my friends. If she could have one or the other donated, she would be able to order from the Albany Food Bank additional frozen or refrigerated food, such as butter and bread, to distribute as needed.

Janet Rock is a person I greatly admire. A friend with a kind heart of gentleness and compassion. A friend who listened and encouraged my endeavors. A friend who, as a secretary at Plattsburgh State University, cared enough to take her lunch hour to type my poems. My friend Janet came to Margot's rescue with an unused chest freezer.

I turned to John for the use of his pickup truck to transport the freezer from Janet's home to Catholic Charities. "Where are we going to get help to move it?," he wondered.

"No problem, we'll go to the Town & Beach Motel and

we'll get Sergio with two other men," I replied.

When we arrived at Janet's, we found it would not fit through the back porch door. "We will get it out," said Sergio as he gave orders in Spanish. He proceeded to pull the nails out of the fastened French-type windows that opened out into a breezeway. It was done so quickly, without the help of my husband, I wondered if Sergio had done this before.

I made a call to Margot's home for her to meet us at the garage at Catholic Charities, and also to let her know we would stop first at McDonalds to treat Sergio and his helpers to breakfast.

Once at the garage they washed and cleaned the freezer thoroughly, making it shine like new. They enjoyed the time away from the boredom of the motel room, but more important, they were doing something useful. Sergio wanted to know if there was anything else they could move or do, for time weighed heavily on them. Unfortunately, the answer was no.

Thanks, Janet, my friend; Margot now has her freezer. It will be put to humanitarian use.

Saturday, October 7

John's and my annual mini-vacation to the seashore fell on the weekend that Parvin left. It could not have come at a better time. I was tired and emotionally drained. An empty, lingering loss not yet numbed by life's reality.

I looked forward to this time with John, taking in the beauty of autumn on our way to one of my favorite places. Searching for inner peace, I walked along the beach to feel, to be touched by, the ever changing sea.

The Seeker

Salty breeze entice my senses;
I am filled with the smells and the taste of your mystic sea.

Once more I return to your sandy shore
In the solitude of a seeker.

I retreat drained to your secluded dunes
Taking rest amid seagrass swaying in the soft breeze.
I seek respite for my emptiness
In the caress of your shifting sands.

I tread along your unmarked wandering beach
With my memories of one who believed
Inspiration is a seed that blooms
In many unexpected ways.

Your rolling waves crest and crash against your shore
With your resounding power and your roar
Wiping my footprints as I pass;
Reclaiming my dreams and returning them to your
    churning sea.

I search the horizon for an omen
And feel your tug at my feet.
My weariness is extracted by your undertow;
My being renewed by your spray.

The depth of my life is felt in my heart
With mysteries of immortality
And I find answers in the beauty
Of your rolling sea.

Monday October 16

Out of the merger of two Plattsburgh Catholic high
schools, Saint John's and Mount Assumption Institute, has
evolved a program which gives students a very real glimpse
of life. It is called the Campus Ministry Program at the newly
formed Seton Catholic Central High School.

The Campus Ministry program, directed by Brother Roland Gaudette and his assistant Ed, visited local nursing
homes, volunteered at the YMCA, and helped senior citizens
with chores at their homes. Brother Roland was looking for
ways to get the program off the ground and he thought of

Catholic Charities, where he might find "something." He and Ed were directed to Margot. She quickly saw how their Campus Ministry might fit in with the Refugee Relief Effort.

With the help of Nancy Monette, librarian at Seton, a food and clothing bank was formed in conjunction with Saint Peter's students and Seton Catholic students. They collected and distributed food, clothing and reading material along with other necessities to the people who fled their homelands.

Under Brother Roland's direction, a Sunday night prayer service was developed with Seton's students providing their own cars to transport the refugees to the school each Sunday evening. After services there were snacks and a time for visiting. "I feel ashamed for what I have," said one senior at Seton when discussing his campus ministry work. "We Americans are spoiled."

Minors traveling on their own had to be placed in the host home network while waiting for their hearing date. Students at Seton welcomed several young men into their midst. The young men lived in the dorm and attended classes at Seton High, taken in under the guiding wings of Seton's students. A very positive experience for the school as well as for their special guests.

The Campus Ministry Program proved itself to be an integral part of the Refugee Relief Effort.

Friday, November 17

November was turning out to be, as last year, a slow month for new arrivals, with only a few days wait for most, while others were here two weeks before entering Canada. Therefore, no plans were made for a Christmas party for the few, mostly non-Christian, refugees. Nonetheless, gifts would be given to those here. It was anticipated, with the political problems in Central America and other countries, that there would be a large influx of refugees in the near future.

Once again, the Brothers of Psi Epsilon Chi Fraternity collected food and money for the Newman Center at Plattsburgh State University. The pastor, Rev. Bill Muench, would make up food baskets for Catholic Charities to distribute to refugee families for Thanksgiving.

Monday, November 20

John and I were looking forward to spending this American feast day with Chris, Mike and our grandchildren. Instead this month will live in my memory as a time of near tragedy, coming by way of a call from Sue Gilman at NYSEG.

It was a time when I was filled with indescribable emotions from disbelief to dismay. A time imprinted with images of dear Margot listening to my nonsensical jabbering, giving of herself with words of encouragement as we drank cups of coffee. She was my anchor in a world that had suddenly gone topsy-turvy.

It was in the latter part of the month that John had a heart attack. By the Grace of God, he was in his office and not out in the field, and I believe that is the reason he is here today. He recognized what was happening and was only ten minutes from the hospital. The quick response of the emergency room medical staff at CVPH Medical Center in administering the experimental drug, TPA (to dissolve the blood clot), caused the "silent killer" to be beaten.

I did not know when or if I would ever return as a volunteer in the Refugee Relief Program at Catholic Charities, only thankful that John had overcome great odds.

Margot, on hearing of John's affliction, borrowed Paul Cote's car, left her work to come to the hospital to be by my side until our son and daughter-in-law arrived from Vermont. She will never fully know how much this meant to me. She was a bright light in my darkened world. Over the following days and weeks she would call to find out how John was progressing, and if we needed anything, "be sure to call."

I had come to know Margot. I found her to be a caring, compassionate lady, not only for the refugees but beyond, in her taking a personal interest in each and every volunteer. For me, and I believe for her, a relationship developed over the years that became more than just a friendly association between a volunteer and her supervisor. It became a relationship in which we spoke intimately about everyday life, with advice when she saw turmoil. She encouraged me, demanding at times more from me in my attempts at poetry, because she knew it was there. I just had to work a little harder, search a little deeper and allow my feelings to be put on paper. Her favorite expression to me, always said with a beautiful smile, was, "Who ever said it would be easy? It isn't meant to be!"

Wednesday, December 20

I had another shock in store when I returned to volunteering in late December (John was doing just fine): Margot told me she would be leaving at the end of the year for a position in the private sector. I was instantly ready to quit, as were Paul and Pat. We had come to truly love this vibrant, vivacious, classy lady. "Fran, I am not leaving Plattsburgh. Stop in and have a cup of coffee with me." It would not be the same. We had grown with the Refugee Relief Program over the years under her tender, loving, care and I would miss her profoundly.

Isle of Refuge, Isle of Love

'Tis a tiny room with picturesque windows
Tucked often a stairwell
Where I am greeted by a lilting voice,
"Hi girl, have a cup of coffee!"
Her smile rivals the morning rays,
Emitting warmth of life that begins the day

181

Where enough pain is felt and seen.

The stark portrait of a warrior from the Far East
Is a reminder I am not immune from life's tragedies.
The oriental wall gallery of folklore masks
Stare in grimacing silence,
Overseeing a desk, a file and three chairs;
This is the volunteer station

Where enough pain is felt and seen.

Her voice becomes rueful in response to a ringing phone
And I see through the facade of buoyancy to her tiredness.
Her silver bracelet jingles
As she searches a paper-strewed desk
For a voucher or perhaps a home for one in exile
In a world he does not understand

Where enough pain is felt and seen.

I saw her bluish-grey eyes illuminate with joy;
Her weariness dispelled as we spoke of the "City of Lights."

Those touched by her compassion in their flight
    from darkness
Hold her in endearment,
For she is their refuge of love remembered
As they begin a renewed life

Where enough pain is felt and seen.

She is a very special lady with energy of three
Finding time as a patron to humble poetry.
She is my mentor I hold in great esteem,
Margo my friend, you are an inspiration to me

And less pain is felt and seen.

(Note: Having not seen Margot's name in writing before composing this
poem, I used strictly phonetic spelling, only learning later that there is a
"t" at the end. However, she and I still use the spelling of Margo, without
a "t," on our correspondence, as a fond remembrance of our first days of
friendship. "T" or no "t," she's still the same wonderful Margot to me!)

Winter, 1989

Thursday, December 21

Although there had not been an organized Christmas party, the Christmas holidays brought an outpouring of love and goodwill with donations of presents and food. Several youth groups helped make Christmas brighter for the refugee children and their families. The youth groups and students from The Church of Jesus Christ of Latter Day Saints, The Bible Baptist Church, Notre Dame Elementary, and Saint Peter's gave gifts. Meredith O'Connor's Chazy Elementary students selected, wrapped and delivered presents to the refugees.

The Hispanic Heritage Club at Plattsburgh Air Force Base organized a "Three Kings" celebration, which included preparing foods, distributing presents and conducting a food and clothing drive.

Seton Catholic Central's Campus Ministry students made plans to host monthly potluck dinners and to regularly visit the refugees in the area as part of their Campus Ministry Program, truly letting people who find themselves "strangers in a strange land" know there are people who care.

Wednesday, December 27

"It's the single largest daily number of refugees we've had since the beginning," a bewildered Brian said, as 40 refugees, mostly women and children from Somalia, crowded into the tiny room at the Crisis Center.

They arrived mid-week just after Christmas. Many dressed in sandals and lightweight clothing in the midst of a cold wave. Peanut butter and jelly sandwiches were served to the Somalian women and children and a few Latin Americans. The lunch left the "jelly shelf" nearly bare.

When Diane Rolfs was interviewed by Mitch Rosenquist of the *Press-Republican*, he asked her, why so many women and children from Somalia?

"They are mostly wives or widows traveling with their children. Before, it was mostly adults and a few children. They're trying to get their children out," she said, adding that "lately there have been women arriving with groups of children who were obviously not their own. I think the women are being paid (by the parents) to just get their children out of the country and they hope to God somebody will take care of them when they get here."

From this dictator-ruled and clan-war-torn country, a woman had to make a choice of which three of her six children would she take to safety. Such was one case Diane told me about and how upset this woman was. A "King Solomon" decision.

With a stay of four weeks or more now, Margot was looking for host homes and food donations. The needs of those arriving with no resources were still being met. However all local resources were being stretched to extremes. As Diane said, "We can't put a woman and six children out on the street." In all, 52 refugees were processed and placed in housing during the week between Christmas and New Year's.

For the year of 1989, a total of 729 refugees had arrived in Plattsburgh, with December seeing the largest number, 107.

Friday, December 29

The volunteer drivers were delighted when Margot told us that at the end of December Maggie Talcott would be replacing her. We had thought we weren't going to see Maggie again! Maggie had finished her studies and would graduate in January with a Bachelors Degree in Human Services.

Resto Chez Lemaire
2095 Route 122
St-Cyrille, Québec
Canada J1Z 1B5
Tél. 819-473-0031 Fax 819-473-0130
resto.serge-lemaire@ca.ca

Facture   X36/50
No compliant   Date 2006-10-22 12:34
Serveuse Danyl   Geste 001

2 avec frites   5.95$H
avec frites   6.99$H
Regulier   1.25$H

1   13.19$
TPS   0.85$ TPS
TVP   1.13$ TVP

11 $ 16.17$ 11 $

Reçu   20.00$

Paiement Cpt   450351   20.00

3 items   Remettre   3.83$

Du solde: 0.00   [0.00]

Maggie was familiar with the many facets of the program, since she had been involved in the relief program almost from the beginning. She was a soft-spoken young lady with a warm bubbly personality. Paul, Pat, Sue and I, were pleased to have her as our new supervisor. It gave us a feeling of continuity of family under her capable guidance.

1990

Tuesday, January 16

As we started the new year, Diane was informed about the fate of the Québec man, LaBlond, the one who had tried to buy the Somalian woman's baby a year earlier.

The Royal Canadian Mounted Police had sent a letter to Police Chief Leo Connick of Plattsburgh, thanking his department, especially patrolmen Daniel Johnson, Wayne Spinks and Alan Ubl for their work on the case and their assistance in the R.C.M.P. investigation. They also thanked District Attorney Penelope D. Clute, for her cooperation.

Under the Canadian Child Protection Law, LaBlond had been charged with four counts of attempting to procure the adoption of a child without consulting the Minister of Health and Social Services. As a result, LaBlond had been convicted and fined in Québec.

Last year, District Attorney Penelope D. Clute had asked for and received arrest warrants. One charged LaBlond with two misdemeanors: attempted unlawful placing of a child out for adoption, and attempted payment for the placement of a child. The other warrant was issued for failing to appear in court January 7, 1989, forfeiting the one hundred dollar bail LaBlond had posted. If he ever comes to the Plattsburgh area, he will be arrested on those warrants.

Sunday, January 21

Two years ago, in 1988, and several times since, Sarah Leen, a freelance photographer for the *National Geographic*, had come to Plattsburgh, spending several days each time. She had been drawn here by the now nationally known Refugee Relief Program. Sarah took pictures, with pre-approval from the them, of the refugees at the Crisis Center, at Darlene's health clinic, at lunchtime at Our Lady of Victory, and while riding with me and at motels. Last year a senior writer for the *National Geographic*, Priit J. Vesilind, came to Plattsburgh to interview people and agencies involved with the program.

The following is an excerpt from the *Press-Republican* of January 20, 1990 under the heading "Of Interest."

> In a feature article on U.S.-Canada relations, the February issue of National Geographic reported on the Plattsburgh Crisis Center and the local chapter of the Salvation Army for their effort during the refugee crisis.
>
> The article elaborates on many of the social, political and economic interactions along the U.S.-Canadian border. Emphasizing the importance of Plattsburgh as a geographical gateway for refugees into Canada, the magazine said "Plattsburgh was America at its best, the people said. But others seemed confused to see America with thousands camped along its border trying to get out."
>
> Interviewed for the article, Brian Smith praised the generosity of local residents and businesses. He said the influx of refugees into the City of Plattsburgh passed the 3,500 mark last year with many of the refugees arriving with no outerwear and few belongings.

Wednesday, January 31

On returning from the border to wait for their entry date, many would ask me in broken English, "Where am I?" At times women would start to cry as I transported them to the

Crisis Center to start their process. All they knew was their flight from terror to a free country named Canada, only to be turned back with a date they did not fully understand. Their eyes held fear of the unknown with thoughts of being deported. "What will happen to me?"

Many disliked the status of "refugee." They would say "I am not a refugee!" Even though they met the criteria for this status they did not like what it inferred. But they had to claim it in order for Canada to allow them entry. For many the status devastated their self-esteem and stripped them of their dignity.

This morning I was at the Sundance to pick up new arrivals. A man in his mid-thirties, from the Middle East, was the first to board the van, taking the passenger's seat next to me. I hardly had my "good morning" out when his eyes filled with tears. He then blurted out words that dismayed me.

"Before my eyes, my wife and children were violated. Then shot." All I could say was, "Oh God!" He went on to tell me how he had lost his business due to the war, therefore he was unable to pay the "demanded" money to a certain faction within the city. I sat stunned as he continued with this horrifying crime: "They came to my house. They tied my hands behind my back when they found I had no money to give them. They forced me to watch as they destroyed my family, my life, before my eyes! They were Moslem as I am. Why?" And I had no answers, only his words imprinted in my mind.

I hoped, with a few days of rest from the fatigue of stressful travel, that he would find what thousands of others have found who passed this way. For it is here, in this little city, "showing America at its best," where many first felt the easing of their pain. They fall in love with this "city of refuge" and the caring people of Plattsburgh. Many wished they could stay and settle here. But for this man I will never know, for I never saw him again. Perhaps he went to stay with friends somewhere in the United States while waiting for his hearing date.

I have seen and heard disturbing stories before over these past years, yet that one was so graphic I shall not forget the pain nor distress that I saw that day.

Wednesday, February 7

"Hi Fran," said Maggie. "Would you be willing to be interviewed by WCFE, Channel 57? I just got off the telephone with Joanne Durfee and she will be calling back within the half-hour to speak with you."

"What is it about, Maggie?"

"They want to do a segment on refugees for North Country Review (a local TV program), which is hosted by Stuart Voss. They want to include an interview of a volunteer's experiences."

"Well, I don't really know if I want to do it, but I am willing to listen and see what it involves. Stuart Voss was one of the first paralegals, wasn't he?"

"Yes. And since you have been in the program from almost the beginning you have knowledge of their emotions and the stress they feel. Also the wonderful friendships you have developed over the years and how important they have become to you." I agreed to be interviewed by Joanne Durfee, producer of the segment.

Sunday, February 11

I made arrangements with Stuart to go to Montréal with the Channel 57 crew, where Stuart would interview Sonia, Merei and Alice for the "Cover Story." Also accompanying Joanne Durfee, Stuart, and the interns from Channel 57 was Program Producer Joann Perry.

Robert, Sonia's husband, who is a master chef, had prepared a banquet for everyone. After the feast, Stuart and the crew left to interview another family in Montréal from a different part of the world. John and I spent the rest of the day and evening with our friends.

Friday, February 23

Tonight, North Country Review, the local interest program on Channel 57, aired its program focused on the North Country's involvement with the refugees. The segment was a thoughtful, sensitive look at the impact that the refugees have, in turn, made on those with whom they came in contact. Both families voiced similar memories of the warmth and kindness they found in Plattsburgh.

Also appearing and interviewed by Stuart were Margot, our former volunteer coordinator; Rolando, a paralegal advisor; and Marie LaCroix, refugee claimant worker for the Committee D'Aide Refugees in Montréal.

The program ended with Middle Eastern background music playing while showing gifts from Central America and the Middle East that were given to us by our now dear friends.

WCFE received more than the usual number of calls after the broadcast in praise of the program, not only from the Plattsburgh area but Québec, Canada, as well.

Thursday, March 1

Our supply of winter outerwear was becoming depleted, as was the "jelly shelf". The concern and willingness of Plattsburgh State students to become involved upon their return in January was self-evident. Alpha Chi Rho Fraternity brought coats to Catholic Charities and started collecting suitcases and household items for the refugees. The sisters of Phi Sigma Sorority donated over 350 pounds of food which they had collected one weekend. This sure helped to replenish winter coats and the "jelly shelf." Just in time!

We were only a few months into the new year when we saw an increase of people seeking assistance, with 96 in the month of February. There was the exciting news of a baby girl being born to one of the families staying here. She had not been the first baby born here over the years, but like the others she is an American citizen, although the family cannot stay in the United States. If a family were to return to their native country and file a claim of the American birth of their child at the United States Embassy, the federal government would consider their admittance—a long drawn out procedure.

Wednesday, March 7

I have always felt this program was very flexible, that somehow when a wall appeared, the people involved found a way around the barrier. Such was the case when Greyhound bus drivers went on strike. Maggie was confronted, as was Diane at the Crisis Center, with the problem of how to get the people to the border for their hearing dates.

With no questions asked, Paul and I offered to take the people up in the van. Paul and I alternated mornings, with Sue Steuart using her own van on several occasions when there was a large group going and in need of a second van for luggage. It meant picking people up at Sundance Motel at 5:30–6:00 a.m., so as not to miss their hearing dates. If their hearing date was for 8:00 a.m. they had to be there two hours before. The others would wait all morning at the border if their hearing was in the afternoon. The van had to be back in time to start the regular day's work for nine o'clock. Paul and I saw many beautiful sunrises during the month of March, but a toll was being taken on our already over-worked, worn-out van. Due to Charlie McGee (at McGee's Service Station), and his TLC, the van had lasted longer than expected, but there was just so much Charlie could do. "It is good for another five or six months, but if you continue the border trips I can't guarantee beyond two or three months." It was a great relief when at the end of the month Greyhound started making runs through Plattsburgh to Montréal at 3:45 a.m. and 6:40 a.m.

The people with hearings at 8:00 a.m. took a cab from the motel to the bus station to catch the 3:45 a.m. bus, waiting in the cold, dark morning. Those with afternoon hearings did the same, except they took the 6:40 a.m. bus. Greyhound had only two early morning buses scheduled, and one very late in the afternoon.

Monday, March 19

With everyone tired of the long months of winter we were looking forward to spring. For Ismial, who had fallen from a third floor window over a year ago, spring arrived early. He now was well enough to leave the hospital to enter Canada. Truly it was a miracle! It turned out, however, to be a very long day for Brian and Diane of the Crisis Center, for no one was at the border to meet Ismial.

Armed with a rare Prime Minister's Permit issued by the government of Canada which would allowed Ismial to enter, Brian and Diane went to CVPH Medical Center hospital to pick up Ismial. Once there, they collected his medical records, then left for the border, where they spent over an hour with Canadian Immigration. Ismial's case file was pulled and all papers were scrutinized, with Ismial's picture being taken before all were allowed to continue on to Montréal. Brian drove directly to the YMCA, where Ismial would be staying. After checking him in, all three then went to the Canadian agency equivalent to our Social Services. Many hours were spent there, with Diane filling out all the needed papers for Ismial and meeting with the caseworker assigned to him. By the time Brian and Diane arrived back in Plattsburgh, twelve long, tiring hours had passed for these two exceptional, caring people.

Spring, 1990

Thursday, March 22

What wonderful news. Oscar and his family received their "Landed Immigrant" papers after three agonizing years. Yet there was sadness. Oscar had received a call from his daughter Maria that his mother had died after months of illness. How sad; first Parvin's mother, then Cora's, now Oscar's and there was nothing they could do, not even able to give their last respects.

Knowing they had finally been accepted by Canada, Oscar bought into a health food store with other partners. They could now get on more firmly with their lives.

Cora was already making plans to return to El Salvador to visit her daughter, Maria, and her son Oscar Jr. and his wife Marialos, and to meet her new granddaughter she had never seen, Gabriela.

Friday, March 23

"Hello?"

"Hi Fran, this is Mehri."

Mehri was a friend of Parvin whom John and I had met. She and her husband Mohamad had a lovely little boy with jet black hair and black eyes named Mazdak. I had been to see Mehri and Mohamad several times with Parvin. In fact, the last hours I spent with Parvin before taking her home and saying good-by was at Mehri's home. John and I had been invited and gone there several times for dinner since Parvin had left. We always felt very welcome in their home and were treated graciously.

"Hi Mehri, how are you? Have you heard from Parvin?"

"No, but we heard she is very busy with many things. Fran, Mohamad and I would like you and John to come for dinner and celebrate with us our NO RUZ" (New Day/Year). I knew their Persian New Year begins at the time of the equinox, as does the arrival of our spring, about March 21st, and was celebrated over several days.

"Mehri, John and I would be honored to come. Thank you. Will you write the meaning of NO RUZ for me?."

"Yes, I will Fran. See you on Sunday."

We were greeted warmly when we arrived, and so delighted to see other friends there. Dear Akbar and Aram; Parvin's former roommate, Mehran, who was like a younger brother to Parvin, and his lovely wife Sylvia, from France, with their beautiful little girl Theolene. We met a young American woman, Laura, who was a visiting guest and friend

Author with husband at a friend's celebration of No Ruz in Montreal, Québec. Note the traditional Persian table for New Year.

of Aram, from Saint Louis, Missouri. We were pleased to see Shakram, also a friend of Aram.

Mehri's table was laden with many appealing dishes that emitted wonderful aromas. Needless to say, John and I satisfied our ravenous appetites on the delicious Iranian banquet. While having tea after this marvelous meal, I asked Mehri about their New Year. I received additional information from Parvin.

Traditional Persian Table of No Ruz (New Day/Year)

Ten days before the NO RUZ, seeds of Sabzeh (wheat) are put in a container of water for 24 hours; then in a wet cloth for another 24 hours; then placed in a dish and kept covered with a moist cloth for another 24 hours until seeds start to sprout, then uncovered. The Persian table consists of seven objects beginning with the letter "S":

Sabzeh (wheat) The green of the wheat symbolizing: the beginning of the season of spring, with all the beauty it holds of new life.
Seeb (apple) symbolizing health.
Sumac symbolizing fertility, rebirth.
Serkeh (vinegar, as wine is now forbidden) symbolizing joyfulness.
Senjed (a fruit not of the West) this fruit is from the Senjed tree, looked upon as a Holy tree from ancient times. Symbolizing the bringing of the blessing for the coming year.
Seer (garlic) symbolizing resistance and power.
Samanou is a dish prepared of wheat germ, walnuts and peanuts.

And a container of water with goldfish and a dish of colored eggs, symbolizing life.

On NO RUZ day a special dinner of fish, rice and herbs is prepared by, and just for, the family.

These traditions have been handed down through thousands of years and are still practiced today in Iran. The weekend before the beginning of the NO RUZ celebration, people travel to the countryside to gather thorny, dry wood to build individual small bonfires in the front of their homes. On Thursday evening before the NO RUZ, the bonfire is lit and each family member leaps over the fire one after another. This action symbolizes the cleansing from sadness and disease and the purification to good health for the coming year. Many young men set off small firecrackers. A tradition somewhat practiced, but being lost, takes place NO RUZ eve. Men and women cloak themselves in the chador (a long, black robe with a hood that covers their features) and call upon their neighbors. They knock on the door and while waiting for the neighbor to answer to give a small gift, such as cookies, they click two spoons together with no words spoken. [Sounds something like our Halloween.]

Sounds of joyful flutes and tambourines resound two weeks before the NO RUZ as the young musicians wander between and down alleyways of homes playing folk music. They bring the good news of the coming NO RUZ. People come out to dance to the music while others watch from their windows.

Thousands of years ago, so it is written, the NO RUZ was celebrated for thirteen days. It remains so today.

In the era of a reigning king, they celebrated for five days to pay respect to him. First the wealthy came to pay their respect, then the peasants came to pay theirs, except the king gave them gifts.

According to tradition the oldest member of the family gives gifts to the younger generation and all children members. However, gifts may be given among family members, such as coins, according to their means.

Traditionally, twelve days of the celebration are spent calling upon, and being visited by, friends and family.

They in turn reciprocate. On the thirteenth day, family and friends leave their homes, villages or city taking the Sabzeh (wheat) with them, gathering to picnic in groups in a beautiful countryside setting. Perhaps along the banks of a river or near a mountain. They leave the Sabzeh when they depart, out of respect and for what it represented, to become once again part of nature.

Fascinating!

Wednesday, May 23

With the warm weather of late spring we were once again aware of the possible increase of new arrivals and facing the housing crunch we see every year. Once again the motels which provided the refugees with shelter during the winter would become full during summer tourist season and other types of housing had to be found.

Already some host families had contacted Maggie, letting her know they were ready to help out. Maggie would be contacting previous host families and hoped to hear that others would be willing to open their hearts and their homes to these "special" guests. A network of host homes extended across the northern region to central New York and the state of Vermont.

Maggie had written in one of her newsletters:

The assistance that a host family gives their refugee guests is immeasurable. The refugees soon find the host home offers them a safe place to stay with unconditional offers of friendship. Not surprisingly, the sharing is reciprocal; host families have described the special friendships they have made with their guests, many of which continue after refugees have become settled in Canada, and how the cultural, educational and spiritual experience of assisting someone from a different country has enriched their lives.

How true.

Refugee waiting times for hearing dates had become much shorter, with an average wait of one and half weeks, but this could change if the numbers increased dramatically. However, we knew now that the student housing would be available once again at the end of the college year, and with previous host families contacting Maggie it looked good for housing.

The call went out for pots, pans, silverware, etc., to set up the apartments. There never seemed to be enough. Of course some of these items were taken into Canada, although each family was asked to leave everything when they left. Human nature is human nature, no matter what part of the world one comes from.

Friday, June 8

Our Refugee Relief Program received a big boost when Church World Service recognized it as one of their 1990 Asylum Immigration Projects. Through this project, Church World Service provides assistance to those programs which they recognize as serving asylum seekers and immigrants considered to be "at risk." Our relief program was very fortunate to be recognized by this world renowned organization.

Summer, 1990

Thursday, June 21

For months Maggie had been seeking and hoping for a refrigerator to supplement the freezer that Margot had been given. It would be used to allow the order and purchase of perishable food products from the Albany Food Bank, as well as making it possible to accept perishable donations. It would complement the "jelly shelf," which would be good. (There was a trend of increased new arrivals within the first five months of this year, with 331 refugees seeking assistance as compared to 210 in 1989. A disproportionate number, 84 percent in one month, had come from Central America.)

Maggie's prayers were answered by the Saint Vincent de Paul Society in Plattsburgh, with its generous donation and delivery of a brand new refrigerator!

Monday, July 3

As many of you already know, I will be leaving the Refugee Relief Effort because my family is relocating out of the area. Although I have been at Catholic Charities as volunteer coordinator for the program for only a short time, I have been involved with the program for three years. During that time I have met people and experienced situations I will not soon forget.

After three years the refugees are not the big newsmakers they used to be, but the terrors they are fleeing are very much the same as those which appeared in the news. We continue to see men who have had to escaped first, leaving their families in hiding because there were immediate threats on their lives; women fleeing with their children because their husbands have been killed or have disappeared, and children who are being sent out on their own as their parents desperately try to save them from the wars raging in their countries. The stories they tell us are so far removed from our own experiences that we would tend to question these stories if it were not for the scores of people we see who are strangers to each other but yet share the same accounts of human tragedy.

For many of these refugees, Canada is their last hope for refuge and the assistance they receive is crucial while they are waiting for their hearing date. Please continue to give the same wonderful support you have shown me to the next volunteer coordinator, Irene Boire.

With these final thoughts, Maggie said good-bye in her last newsletter in the first month of summer. Paul, Pat and I were disheartened by the news of losing another outstanding, caring volunteer coordinator.

Maggie had been so gentle and compassionate, to the point of tears, in her concern for these despairing people. Yet Maggie, like dear Margot, always had the welfare of her volunteers uppermost in her mind. Her concern for our driving a dying van found her compiling statistics on its usage, searching for and completing a first draft to submit for a grant in hopes of receiving monies toward a new van. However, Maggie had to leave before she could do the final draft.

I was sure she would be successful in her studies for her Master's degree at Boston College. Paul, Pat, Sue and I would miss Maggie very much!

Wednesday, July 11

In early summer a Middle Eastern refugee family was deported from Canada. I had met them the previous summer. Why they were deported I do not know. Perhaps their claim for Refugee Status, according to Canada, was not strong enough. In any case, they called a Plattsburgh resident who became their friend while they were here in 1989. He, in turn, called the Crisis Center. The agency could do nothing for the family, but advised him to seek legal counsel. The friend was told by legal counsel to tell the family to claim U.S. asylum on their arrival at the American Border. Under escort by Canadian authorities, they did just that.

American Immigration was very nice to them in helping them fill out all necessary papers. However, this family is in "limbo," no status, no country, not qualified for any social services and not permitted to work. But they have an exceptional American friend here in Plattsburgh who has taken them under his wing, and into his heart. This is the only case that I am aware of, but I am sure there were others that were deported.

Thursday, July 26

Irene, our new volunteer coordinator, had had contact with refugees through her acquaintance with Celine MacDougall, who hosted. However, I had never met or seen Irene in my three years in the program.

I learned that she had a Bachelor's degree in music and was a very talented young lady. She wrote her own lyrics and music, and played many different instruments. Irene also spoke fluent French and taught French classes twice a week at Clinton Community College.

Irene brought with her many new ideas. We volunteers listened and were more than willing to help her in any way to become familiar with our program. If asked, we would assist in implementing her ideas into the program, for now the program was in her hands.

One idea, which turned out to be quite a surprise, was the arrival of a huge truck filled with thirty-gallon bags of fresh spinach from the gleaning of fields in the Malone area. It came from the Cooperative Gleaning Effort that is administered by the Community Action Agency Effort of Franklin County. Funded by the New York State Department of Health Supplemental Nutritional Assistance Program (SNAP) through a grant designated as Homeless and Destitute Program, workfare participants and those involved in the Summer Youth Program went into the fields and gleaned after the machines had harvested. The program served two counties and hoped to expand in helping those in need.

Even though Irene was looking with the best of intentions for ways to supplement our "jelly shelf" with fresh donated fruit and vegetables, this one unfortunately turned out to be an enormous problem of wilting, dripping, stinking spinach in Our Lady of Victory's brand new walk-in cooler in a matter of one day!

When I checked in late in the day after the spinach had been stored, Steve Patnode, office manager at Catholic Charities, asked if I knew where Irene was. I didn't. He told me he had just received a call from Sister Bernadette at Our Lady of Victory about leaking spinach. I said, "I will check before I go home." I met the janitor at OLV lugging bags of spinach to the dumpster. Needless to say, I knew there was a problem! I climbed into the parked van, went to student housing, picked up three refugee men, and went back to clean out the cooler. At four o'clock, where do you take a van full of smelly spinach? The landfill, which is sixteen miles outside of the city, was closed. We returned to student housing, where we left the dumpster full. On telling Steve what I had done, he said, "Catholic Charities will be willing to pay for the cost of a garbage pick up, if Mr. Meron (he owned the student housing where the refugees were renting) is charged extra."

Irene's intentions were well meaning, but we did not have proper storage facilities for this type of food and at any given time we could be down to just two refugees. She found out she could not give it away to other programs in Plattsburgh as they could not store it adequately either. This was the end of any bulk donations.

Irene felt strongly that the community should be made more aware of the relief program taking place here. Twice she was invited by Kathy Rock, of WKDR Talk Radio, to speak about the program, once with a Panamanian family waiting to enter Canada. I am not aware of the results; I only know and have experienced over the years that people of our North Country have opened their hearts generously in so many ways, and have done so quietly.

Thursday, August 2

What we had hoped would not happen came to pass. Almost to the month that Charlie McGee had predicted, the van quit. Charlie came once more to the rescue, but it would be several days before he would have it back in service. For the first time the Refugee Transportation Program at Catholic Charities had to turn elsewhere for transportation, namely Big Red Taxi, which had offered the best rates.

It soon became apparent how much the volunteer drivers, and the van, were missed. Yet, the final application to be completed so it might be submitted for grant monies toward a new van had not been worked on. On picking up the van Charlie said, "It does not have much longer to run." The drivers were very concerned and becoming frustrated. Charlie could not continue to put band-aids on a dying van, though he somehow managed to get it running once again.

We wondered if the final application for the grant would ever be completed or submitted.

Fall, 1990

Wednesday, September 19

That fall Plattsburgh State University students did not forget the ongoing refugee effort to which they had given so generously in the past years.

Students living in dormitories received welcome packages containing sample sizes of various toiletries. Bill Laundry, Director of Campus Life, with Resident Assistants and volunteers, collected unused samples and donated them to the refugee program. These toiletries were given out as needed to new arrivals. Many refugees arrived without these very basic necessities.

Alpha Phi Gamma Sorority sponsored a refugee food drive, collecting large boxes of food for our "jelly shelf." Whiteface Hall Council, Adirondack Hall Council and Banks Hall Council enjoyed a barbecue cookout together. A large amount of food was left over. They delivered to Catholic Charities untouched packages of hamburger rolls, hot dog rolls and cases of meat. Our freezer was full due to their thoughtfulness. Again, this would be given out to new arrivals as they went through a one or two day process before coming into the program.

These young women and young men from the college once again exhibited their awareness, their caring, toward the despairing strangers in our area.

The First Presbyterian Church and the Wesleyan Church of Hammond joined forces and filled a pick-up truck full of clothes, food, blankets, rice, and honey. They were just in time to help replenish our winter clothing and added to our always used "jelly shelf." These nameless people were giving so much, knowing how crucial their assistance was to this program for refugees as they waited to enter Canada. And caring enough to travel one hundred sixty miles to deliver all these much-needed items!

Saturday, October 6

On a gorgeous autumn day, I stopped at the Sundance to see if the young couple from Bulgaria, Stephanie and her husband George (we were beginning to see Eastern European refugees), would like to attend the Saint Francis Festival. It was sponsored by Saint Peter's Church, in collaboration with other area churches, to be held at Clinton Community College, Lake Shore Road, Route 9 South. When I told Winnie, owner of the Sundance, where we were going, she asked if she could come. "Sure, the more the merrier," I replied.

Located on a high bluff, the college overlooks Lake

Champlain and the magnificent Green Mountains of Vermont to the east. To the west are the majestic mountains of our Adirondacks. It is a very picturesque, peaceful setting.

Catholic Charities had been invited to participate and Irene was to bring and display refugee photos or memorabilia. Catholic Charities Refugee Program would benefit and share along with the Plattsburgh Interfaith Food Shelf, Champlain Valley Birthright, Saint Benedict's, Buffalo (serving AIDS victims), and Ronald McDonald House in Burlington, Vermont from proceeds brought in from the day's events.

The admission was free (donations if you wished) with a program of events that was outstanding. It quickly became evident that many people had worked very hard, with many hours invested for this fun-filled day. There were arts and crafts for sale, music from jazz to country/western, choirs, classical music and much more. Sister Mary Felicitas Wells, who had been a devoted volunteer at the shelter, was overseeing the refugee display table. It was so nice to see and visit with this kind lady after so many months.

Stephanie and her husband George loved it, as did Winnie and I, as we strolled around the lovely college grounds, taking in the events. The friendly people, the music and the setting made for a perfect day. A day we did not want to come to an end.

Tuesday, October 23

It seemed like many changes were taking place in late fall, but once again this program showed how flexible it had become and we volunteers took it all in stride.

Brian Smith had left the Crisis Center for a new position. After many weeks, in early October, Faith Shields was hired as new director of the Crisis Center. I liked her right away, with her warm "hello" and friendly smile.

After weeks of problems the van again died. I mean it would not move! The transmission was gone. We were forced, once again, to utilize Big Red Taxi, with the cost draining the private grant funds of the relief program of Catholic Charities.

Irene was given an old, rusty 16–passenger 1981 van by Tom Wood. We felt elated! We had a van that ran well, we thought. However, that lasted only two weeks before the transmission gave out.

Thursday, November 1

Keeper Of Time

My heart is a timekeeper waiting for the dawn of your hello
That will lift my veil of darkness of your good-bye.
Through misty eyes I search the heavens for your
    namesake
And find the silent night lit by my thoughts of you.

Yet, I find joy in my secluded sorrow
In remembering the cherished days spent with you.
An interlude of a loving friendship
That captures my heart between your hello and good-bye.

The vivid days instilled forever
With photos of you printed in my mind.
My evenings echo with your melodious songs
And time flies on wings into the night.

I have harvested from your field of joy
Reaping the happiness that nourishes my life.
I have seen your tears of despair that touched
  the core of my soul.

I have consumed the fruit from your tree of knowledge
And my being flourishes with the love of understanding.
Bonded by these memories our unity spans the universe
For I am a keeper of time
Waiting for the dawn of your shining smile
And to know once more the warmth of your embrace.

Parvin returned on a day I shall never forget, my birthday! Akbar had called earlier in the day to tell me she was to arrive in Montréal that evening. When Parvin called later that night and I heard her happy but tired voice, I began to believe she was truly back. We had, over the past many months, exchanged letters and phone calls, but they never really filled the void I had always felt.

Several days later, on my way to see Parvin for the first time in more than a year, with the miles seemingly dragging by, I wondered if our friendship had changed. After all, it had been a long time, and people's feelings do change.

When I finally arrived and saw her, I knew I was no longer a "keeper of time" waiting for the return of one who believes in and teaches "to seek the inner beauty of life"—a belief that leaves her vulnerable to the real world of pain. One who aspired to instill the advice, "to know yourself, then you will know life." One who inspired an awakening within me that enables me to express the joy and the sorrow I have seen and felt in a way I never dreamed possible. With words lost in happiness, it was the reunion of a unique friendship, one life complementing the other filling our hearts with joy.

Welcome back, Parvin Jon (an endearment): my friend.

Friday, November 16

Having worked as Volunteer Coordinator for five, hectic months, Irene left, taking a private job in the educational community and leaving Steve Patnode, office manager at Catholic Charities, to take on the additional burden as our volunteer coordinator.

Steve did not hesitate to turn to his seasoned volunteers or Diane at Crisis Center for advice. He was there for the volunteers if we had to call in while on the road, which happened occasionally, for his needed advice or approval. It was very important to have, and to be able to contact, the coordinator, for problems do arise. Steve proved not only to be a quick learner of the program, but considerate and interested as to how the volunteer's day had gone, which we had felt was missing over the past months. Added to all of this, Steve had a quick wit and a great sense of humor, with a contagious laugh. A great asset, to my way of thinking, that was needed in this position.

Meanwhile the search was on for a new volunteer coordinator.

Wednesday, December 5

Word had gone out about the van and our desperate situation. Enough donated monies were received by early December to fix our original van, which would take time to repair. A period of three weeks elapsed, during which Big Red Taxi did the transporting. It was a large expense. Nonetheless, Pat, Paul, and I, on days we were to volunteer, met the taxi van at Sundance and went with the refugees to do their grocery shopping. Many did not speak English, and therefore did not understand the voucher or how to check out.

Sunday, December 9

John and I went to Montréal with our Christmas gifts earlier than usual in December to visit our friends. Not only to remember them in the upcoming holiday season, but to welcome Cora back from her visit to El Salvador. We also were carrying an invitation, on behalf of our daughter-in-law Mike, to invite Parvin to spend Christmas day with our family.

The hours flew as we first visited Sonia, Robert and family, then on to Oscar, Cora and family, where we received all the news about Maria. Our last stop, having also been invited by Mehri and Mohamad, was to partake in the celebration of Mazdak's second birthday.

On our arrival at Mehri's, we were greeted by many familiar faces and friends. It was a very pleasing way to end a busy day, eating and visiting with Parvin, Aram, Akbar, Lila, and her husband Akbar, as well as with the many others present. I relayed Mike's invitation to Parvin along with John's and my invitation to spend extra days with us if possible. Parvin was receptive and delighted by the invitations.

(The refugees had not been forgotten on our American feast day, Thanksgiving. Captain Edgar George of the Salvation Army and his staff, invited the refugees to partake along with the many local people they feed every year. Again, the Salvation Army showed their unhesitating willingness to help.)

Winter, 1990

Thursday, December 20

For the refugees' Christmas celebration in Plattsburgh, Father Bill Muench (John XXIII Newman Center) and his parish donated a large number of roasting chickens. This enabled Catholic Charities to provide every refugee household with a makeshift Christmas dinner, supplemented with other donated foods and fresh fruit purchased, with donated monies, from the Kiwanis Club of Plattsburgh. Alan Woo, owner of Wong Kwon, a Chinese restaurant on Margaret Street, donated one hundred pounds of rice to be divided and added to the Christmas baskets.

Meredith, a longtime friend of the refugees, arranged a canned food collection at her school, Chazy Central Rural School, in December which netted approximately 500 pounds of food for the program. As an incentive to her elementary students to bring in food, Meredith baked, constructed and raffled a gingerbread house, reaping a huge success for her special effort.

So that the children of refugees could have a small Christmas gift (a party had not been planned), a local couple, Ron and Dee Black from nearby Peru, brought in coloring books and crayons to be given out.

To pack and deliver the Christmas dinner baskets, with the brightly wrapped gifts, friends from the Adirondack Residential Center in Schuyler Falls volunteered their time. Five young residents from the center, Josh, Jon, Wally, Luke and Jon, along with a teacher, Jerry Ross, were Santa's helpers for Catholic Charities this year.

Monday, December 31

An excerpt from Steve's newsletter:

It is important to mention here all the small but essential individual donations which arrived throughout the holiday season from anonymous donors who stopped in just long enough to drop off a bag of food, mittens, or toys. These touching gestures of thoughtfulness are the lifeblood of this program.

As we came to the end of the year there was an increase of people needing assistance, with 28 arriving within a three day period in November, and December saw 65 more. A total of 807 for 1990, an increase of 10 percent from last year.

Of the thousands who have spent weeks or months here, only one case, involving a young refugee man, marred an up-to-now clean record of no serious problems. In the latter part of this year he entered a private residence and stole some jewelry. His case is still pending as this year comes to an end.

In December, a lovely young lady named Tatiana, from Sofia, Bulgaria, wrote of the traditional Bulgarian Christmas. This young architect was honored to share her memories when asked how her holiday season was celebrated.

In the afternoon of the 24th of December, is prepared the Christmas tree. It was bought one or two days before, and is an Alder tree. It will be decorated with Christmas balls and Christmas bells, various small toys, garlands, and candles (or garland of small lamps).

Over the tree is put a special toy called "top or star" to finish the whole decoration. The children take part in the decoration. It is a big experience for them. The mother (or another woman in the family) knits the Christmas wreath from fresh Alder-twigs, and decorates it with garland, balls, fir-cones, candles and bow. The Christmas wreath will be hung on a lamp at the wall, or will be put in the middle of the Christmas table.

For dinner a special meal is prepared, completely without meat or grease. For example: rice wrapped in cabbage sheets, dry red peppers, stuffed with beans and walnuts; sour salads, from grated turnips and pickles; a soup-like, made from dry fruits such as: pieces of apple, pear, plum, quince, orange-rind.

For dessert, special sweets are prepared that will remain until the New Year; a special pastry with squash and another pastry that is very sweet, with walnuts; boiled wheat with walnuts that has Turkish origin.

At seven or eight o'clock, all the family is around the Christmas table. All the plates are on the table. The mother prepared a handmade-bread, the Christmas bread. It is in the middle with the wreath. On the bread is a candle brought from the church.

This table must be as rich as the nature. All members of the family stand around and the eldest sanctifies the food with a icon-lamp, that he shakes over. Everyone makes the sign of the cross. After that they sit down and start dinner. The Christmas candles are not blown out, they burn out, this is to make the coming year healthy.

The holiday of 24th of December, is a family holiday. In the midnight, the Grand Father Frost, is coming. He takes the presents and puts them under the Christmas tree or nearby the children's beds. When they wake-up, they find a surprise.

On the morning of the 25th of December, the family goes

to church (by now that was impossible). In the afternoon and evening the family gets and makes good-wishes to the feast. They entertain guest, close friends, neighbors or relatives or go as guest of others. The principle is—the youngsters have to go to the elders.

People with names—Kristo, Kristina, Kristalina, and others—have a Name day, and are entertained too. Everyone enjoys himself.

Children prepared in the days before, a special Christmas twig. They would hit the elder-relatives (lightly) with the twig on the back, sing carols and wish them health and success for the next year. The relatives give the children petty cash (coin or 1, 2, to 5 leva).

Everyone can now sit down to a special meal of turkey, with cabbage stuffed with rice. Sometimes this meal can be served in the New Year night too. So, the Christmas tree is lit, all are happy.

The holiday continues a long time into the night.

Tatiana wrote this using only her English/Bulgarian dictionary, which took her three days.

1991

Tuesday, January 1

The Saturday before Christmas, Parvin had arrived at our home thanks to Akbar's kindness in driving her here in his car. We were sorry that Akbar could only stay over one night before he had to return home. John and I always enjoyed his friendliness and the humor he showed to those around him. He indeed was a good friend.

Parvin enjoyed our Christmas holiday immensely, which we spent celebrating with our son Chris and his family in Vermont. Christmas is made special by children, in an atmosphere charged with their anticipation of Santa's arrival. It was a joy watching them carefully arrange the snack of milk, cookies and carrots for Santa and his hardworking reindeer, before retiring for the longest night of their young lives.

We prepared Parvin for the children's early morning rise, and their rush to see if Santa had stopped by. However, when I went downstairs to make coffee she was already up, and had been since 6:00 a.m. When the children came down they found Santa had left presents under the tree for them, as well as gifts for their mom and dad from Parvin. Santa also had left gifts for Parvin as well.

That evening Parvin had an added adventure. On our trip by ferry to Vermont, Lake Champlain had been quiet; however, it wasn't quiet on our return home with the large rolling waves. She was quite happy when we finally docked! The rest of the week was spent doing what so many women love to do, shopping. (This writer excluded, but along I went!)

On the last day of December we brought Parvin home, bringing with us Oscar and family's forgotten Christmas gift. On New Year's Eve we were on our way to Oscar's when we had a car accident at an intersection in Montreal. Fortunately, no one was hurt, but where do you turn, who do you call when you are in another country, much less on New Year's Eve, and New Year's Day being a holiday? Now I felt what it meant to be in a foreign country with nowhere to turn. It was Oscar and Cora who came to our rescue, to our aid. And the meaning of the phrase, "what goes around comes around" was illustrated. I must say how helpful the constables are in Montréal with their translation and suggestions.

Cora and Oscar took us under their wings, bringing us to their home for the night. Erika and Sandra gave us their beds for what turned out to be a sleepless night. Their telephone was at our disposal for any calls we needed to make, one being to my friend, Mary Jane. Once again, she was there for me, contacting a local towing company and calling back with the information. The next day, Oscar took us to the place where our car had been towed. Thank goodness for Oscar's French (we do not speak a word), for he helped with settling the cost with the French-speaking towing company. Mary Jane has been a dear friend I could always count on for over 25 years, but Oscar and Cora were also there for us when we did not know where to turn. We shall never forget their kindness or the beginning of 1991.

Freedom

The strength of this word
Rings the globe with a burning desire
That incites hearts and souls
Thirsting to break the chains of bondage.

From the steamy jungles to fervent desert lands
They march to the beat of freedom,
With passionate voices chanting as one
A living wave surging in quest of the revered mecca.

The beat grows into a thunderous roar
Not to retreat from tyranny,
Unafraid and naked for all to see
They stand before the world to be counted.

For a moment in time mankind knows
The bittersweet taste of freedom
Until the cry is silenced by a gun
And life's red wine flows for liberty.

Toll the bell slowly
For the obscene stain on mother earth.
Know the precious quest will not be purged
For the human spirit is cast in the legacy of freedom.

In the last three years the refugees have come from 54 countries around the world, including Russia. Our latest influx of people was from Eastern European countries such as Bulgaria, Czechoslovakia and Romania and a few from Russia. We also had families from Kuwait and Jordan in December.

They are not all from low economic levels. Some are doctors, lawyers, teachers and people from all walks of life with one thing in common. They can't stay where they're from and are doing their best to stay alive.

Frightened and confused, they arrive in Plattsburgh to be greeted by the warm hospitality of the people from the North Country, caring agencies and the interdenominational relief effort. They in return give their only gift—their love.

There are so many caring people from all over the northeast, across the United States and even Canada, who have given through the years.

The pick-up truck filled with donations that still makes its once a year trip from downstate; the five dollar check for the refugee fund given by one on fixed income; the churches of all denominations far and wide, holding bake sales to raise money; the Armed Force's clubs making drives for donations; the fraternities and sororities at Plattsburgh State University who collected canned goods; all giving, whether large or small, from their heart in support of these refugees seeking freedom.

You are all remembered each time a bag of rice, a can of soup, some fresh produce, a coat or sweater, a pair of mittens, or a simple toy is given out. We, the volunteers, are the lucky ones when we hear, "Merci," "Muchas Gracias," "Showkrann," or "Thank You!"

The passage over these past three years has been a testament to both the tenderness of the human heart and the strength of the human soul.

I met the Latinos who approach life with humor and laughter.

I faced the young man who said, "Look at me and see Africa," and I gazed upon a continent in turmoil.

214

I've read Hafiz and viewed the Tonbak, Kamancheh, Santour, Tar, Se-tar and the lonely Nay in concert and I am touched by ancient Persia.

I've gathered treasured friendships.

I have met the remnants from the slayers of spirits, and they have become my images.

Postscript

In June 1992 the Canadian Parliament introduced, and passed, Bill C-86. This bill gave Canadian customs officials more power to determine on their own who could and could not enter Canada for asylum at the time the person seeking refugee status arrived at the border.

The new law was implemented February 1, 1993. Refugees were either admitted immediately into Canada to wait for a hearing date, or deported immediately if deemed unacceptable. The new policy thus eliminated the waiting period in Plattsburgh which the Refugee Relief Effort was created to support. On April 30, 1993, this most remarkable program ceased operation.

Erika graduated from high school in June 1991 and continued her studies at Vanier College in Montréal. She married

The wedding of Jamie, escorted by her proud dad, Marcel, in Montreal, Québec, where the author and husband were guests. 1991.

in April of 1993 and now lives in Greenbelt, Maryland. Sandra graduated from high school in June 1993. Oscar, Cora and Sandra returned to El Salvador, after receiving their Canadian citizenship in 1993, feeling it is safe due to the signing of a peace treaty between the El Salvadoran government and the guerrillas. Erika also received her Canadian citizenship in 1994.

Jamie married in August of 1991 and continues to work as secretary-receptionist at the same law office. Her mother Theresa is attending language classes. Her father Marcel is working. Jamie's youngest sister Merei graduated from high school and is continuing her studies. Theresa, Jamie's oldest sister, is married. All are now Canadian citizens.

Sonia and Robert are still working fourteen hour days, seven days a week, but for themselves. In July 1993 they bought and now operate their own restaurant. Their dreams are finally coming true. Merei is taking classes at Vanier College in Montréal, to become an anesthesiology assistant. Alice graduated from high school in June, 1991, and is now taking classes in Computer Science at McGill Univerity in Montréal. The family became Canadian citizens in 1994.

Parvin enrolled at, and graduated from, Shadd Academy with a degree in accounting in May of 1992. She went to Toronto, Ontario to look for employment, returning to Montréal in the late fall. With no jobs available she returned home to Iran to visit family and friends, but will return to Canada. Parvin received her Canadian citizenship in 1991.

Rolando Miranda is teaching Spanish classes at Plattsburgh State University. "It is a time for them to rest without fear," he had said about the refugees in Plattsburgh.

Darlene Edwards, who once "wished to join the Peace Corps," ran the Health Department Refugee Clinic until the program closed in April of 1993. She submitted reports every six months to the Health Department. "I only remarked on the remarkable. But I never knew what the day was going to bring," she said. Darlene is back full time as a county health nurse.

Diane Rolfs used her many talents in her job out of concern for new arrivals. "If these people could stay in their homeland, they would. They would love to go home." Diane accepted a position in the educational field in late 1990.

Peter Bertoia began January 1991 as the new Refugee Support Services Coordinator at the Crisis Center. He was a native of Toronto, Canada, who brought to the position the ability to speak French. He also held a Bachelor's Degree. However, Peter had to leave after only a few months on the job, for he could not receive a working permit for employment in the United States.

Jane Alexander replaced Peter Bertoia. Jane held a Bachelor's Degree from SUNY at Plattsburgh. She was the Coordinator for the Crisis Center until the refugee program closed in April of 1993. She then took a position with Social Services in Plattsburgh.

Cliff Byrne became the new Volunteer Coordinator of Refugee Services at Catholic Charities and was somewhat familiar with the program. Cliff, who has a Master's Degree, had just completed an eight-month graduate counseling internship at Catholic Charities. Starting in early January of 1991, Cliff brought new energy and enthusiasm to the program. He served as Volunteer Coordinator until the program closed.

Paul Cote retired from driving the van, due to ill health, in 1990. His wife Pat, however, continued until the closing of the program. Two dedicated volunteers who were an integral part of the Refugee Relief Program.

Sue and Bernie Steuart did "God's work with love,"

perhaps not as often as at the beginning, but nevertheless they drove when called upon. Sue did a lot anonymously, without fanfare. Her many trips to Montréal, helping those less fortunate, remain untold and unpublished.

List of Countries From Which Refugees Have Fled

Latin America: Argentina, Bolivia, Brazil, Chile, Colombia, Ecuador, Surinam, Peru, El Salvador, Guatemala, Honduras, Nicaragua, Venezuela, Panama, Mexico.

Africa: Djibouti, Egypt, Ethiopia, Gambia, Guinea, Ivory Coast, Liberia, Nigeria, Somalia, South Africa, Sudan, Zaire.

Asia: Afghanistan, Bangladesh, India, Pakistan.

Middle East:Iran, Iraq, Israel, Lebanon, Jordan, Kuwait, South Yemen, Syria, Yemen.

Europe: France.

Eastern Europe: Bulgaria, Czechoslovakia, Hungary, Poland, Romania, Soviet Union.

Indian Ocean: Seychelles, Sri Lanka.

Pacific: Philippines.

Caribbean: Bahamas, Cuba, Dominican Republic, Trinidad.